STRIKE
THE ORIGINAL
Match

BIBLE STUDY GUIDE

From the Bible-teaching ministry of

Charles R. Swindoll

INSIGHT FOR LIVING

Charles R. Swindoll is a graduate of Dallas Theological Seminary and has served as senior pastor of the First Evangelical Free Church of Fullerton, California, since 1971. Chuck's radio program, "Insight for Living," began in 1979. In addition to his church and radio ministries, Chuck enjoys writing. He has authored numerous books and booklets on a variety of subjects.

Based on the outlines and transcripts of Chuck's sermons, the study guide text is co-authored by Lee Hough, a graduate of the University of Texas at Arlington and Dallas Theological Seminary. He also wrote the Living Insights sections.

Editor in Chief:
Cynthia Swindoll

Coauthor of Text:
Lee Hough

Assistant Editor:
Wendy Peterson

Copy Editors:
Deborah Gibbs,
Glenda Schlahta

Production Artists:
Renee Dallas,
Gary Lett

Typographer:
Bob Haskins

Director, Communications Division:
Deedee Snyder

Project Manager:
Alene Cooper

Project Supervisor:
Susan Nelson

Project Assistant:
Ellen Galey

Print Production Manager:
John Norton

Printer:
Sinclair Printing Company

Unless otherwise identified, all Scripture references are from the New American Standard Bible, © The Lockman Foundation 1960, 1962, 1963, 1968, 1971, 1972, 1973, 1975, 1977. Used by permission. The other translation cited is The Living Bible [LB].

An effort has been made to locate sources and obtain permission where necessary for the quotations used in this book. In the event of any unintentional omission, a modification will gladly be incorporated in future printings.

ISBN 0-8499-8438-6
Printed in the United States of America.
COVER DESIGN: Paul Showalter
COVER PHOTOGRAPHY: Fewsmith Photography

CONTENTS

*These messages were not a part of the original series but are compatible with it.

INTRODUCTION

The deterioration of marriages today is a painful reality that has led to bruised lives and broken homes. The tragic results have reached epidemic proportions even among Christians in the church.

Because God originated the first "match," having drawn up the initial plans for the home, it makes good sense for us to return to Him for counsel and direction. That's what makes these messages so vital—they are based squarely on the most reliable source of information regarding the husband-wife relationship, God's Word . . . the Bible.

Not until we return to Scripture and reorder our lives according to the pattern set forth in its pages will we be able to rekindle the fire that has grown cold in many marriages. I pray that the Lord will use this study to start that process in homes today where recovery seems remote at best and restoration merely a distant dream.

Chuck Swindoll

PUTTING TRUTH INTO ACTION

Knowledge apart from application falls short of God's desire for His children. He wants us to apply what we learn so that we will change and grow. This study guide was prepared with these goals in mind. As you go through the following pages, we hope your desire to discover biblical truth will grow as your understanding of God's Word increases, and that you will be encouraged to apply what you've learned.

To assist you in your study, we've included a section called Living Insights at the end of each lesson. These exercises will challenge you to study further and to think of specific ways to put your discoveries into action.

There are many ways to use this guide—in personal devotions, group studies, discussions with friends and family, and Sunday school classes. And, of course, it's an ideal study aid when you're listening to its corresponding "Insight for Living" radio series.

To benefit most from this study guide, we would encourage you to consider it a spiritual journal. That's why we've included space in the Living Insights for recording your thoughts and discoveries. We hope you'll return to those sections often for review and encouragement as you continue to grow in your walk with Christ.

Lee Hough
Coauthor of Text
Author of Living Insights

STRIKE
THE ORIGINAL
Match

Chapter 1

LET'S CONSULT THE ARCHITECT

Genesis 2:18–25; Proverbs 24:3–4

Can you imagine building a home without an architect's carefully drawn plans? The kitchen sink might end up in the dining room, and the living room would probably have the washer and dryer connections sticking out of the fireplace. And who knows about the wiring. Flip the light switch on in the master bedroom and the oven would start to preheat. Not the kind of place where you would want to spend the rest of your life.

No reasonable person would think of building a home without the carefully drawn plans of an architect. And yet, people regularly attempt to build their marriages without consulting the Master Architect of that divine institution. We rely instead on the sketchy blueprints we receive from our parents, our friends, and the world around us. The result is two people under the same roof hammering away to build a model marriage based on two different sets of plans.

Sound confusing? It is. That's why so many couples end up with such poorly constructed marriages. Take a close look and you'll see that their love has faded, their commitment is crumbling, the communication is wired all wrong, the foundation is cracked, and the roof's sagging and about to cave in. Not the kind of marriage where people would want to spend the rest of their lives.

And so many don't. They choose instead to have their marriages condemned and bulldozed under. Don't let anybody fool you, though; divorce is painful, humiliating, a nightmare. But so is living in a neglected, poorly designed marriage. What can we do?

We can put away our amateur ideas of how to build a good marriage and start remodeling based on the blueprint found in God's Word. It won't be easy; we're not going to tell you, "Trust

God and your remodeling will work out happily ever after." Rebuilding is not that simple. In fact, anybody who has remodeled a house knows that

- it takes longer than you planned,
- it costs more than you figured,
- it is messier than you anticipated,
- it requires greater determination than you expected.

Remodeling a marriage isn't any different. It, too, will probably take longer, cost more, be messier, and require greater determination than you expected. But the reward, the blessing of building according to God's design—now that promises to be the kind of marriage where you'll want to spend the rest of your life!

Introduction to the Series

Though this study may be more interesting and timely for those who are or will soon be married, it can still be encouraging and enriching for the single person. Studying God's Word is always profitable. We should also mention that this is essentially a biblical study. Although bookstores are lined with books on the family and the home, few of them focus primarily on biblical passages. All the way through, we plan to draw our insights and applications from Scripture.

Observations from Scripture

Before we begin swinging our hammers and knocking down walls, however, let's consult the Master Architect's original plans for marriage in Genesis 2.

Genesis 2:18–25

Genesis opens with the world under construction. God is busy framing mountains and seas, birds and beasts, light, stars, sea creatures, and grass, trees, and flowers. You know that He is pleased with His handiwork as you read the account because He repeatedly steps back, looks it over, and says it is "good" (Gen. 1:4, 10, 12, 18, 21, 25, 31). When you reach Genesis 2:18, however, you find the Lord saying for the first time that something is *not* good.

> Then the Lord God said, "It is not good for the man to be alone." (v. 18a)

In Hebrew, the negative used here is even more emphatic: "**not good,** this aloneness of man." The word *aloneness* means that Adam was isolated; that something was missing, incomplete in his life. What he needed was "a helper suitable for him" (v. 18b). The Lord knew this, but He waited until Adam had discovered it for himself before He took action (vv. 19–20). Then He graciously went to work creating a suitable helper He knew Adam would think was good—very good!

> So the Lord God caused a deep sleep to fall upon
> the man, and he slept; then He took one of his ribs,
> and closed up the flesh at that place. And the Lord
> God fashioned into a woman the rib which He had
> taken from the man. (vv. 21–22a)

The word *fashioned* literally means "build or rebuild." God rebuilt Adam's rib into a counterpart who would help him find the fulfillment and completion he lacked in his aloneness. Then came the exciting moment when the Lord gave away the bride.

> And [He] brought her to the man. And the man said,
> "This is now bone of my bones,
> And flesh of my flesh;
> She shall be called Woman,
> Because she was taken out of Man."
> (vv. 22b–23)

To read this without understanding the emotion communicated in the Hebrew, you might think Adam was incredibly dull and deadpan. But actually quite the opposite was true. He was joyously astonished when he saw Eve—his first words were literally, "Now, now at last, at long length!" He knew immediately that he had been given the suitable helper he needed so desperately. The Living Bible translates his first words as, "This is it!" Don't let the serious-sounding "bone of my bones, flesh of my flesh" fool you; Adam was one excited fellow. He was happy—God had created something good, very good.

And what follows this groom's first sight of his bride is God's blueprint for marriage.

> For this cause a man shall leave his father and his
> mother, and shall cleave to his wife; and they shall
> become one flesh. And the man and his wife were
> both naked and were not ashamed. (vv. 24–25)

The Hebrew term for *cleave* means "to glue" or "to glue one's self." From this verse we see that the husband and wife are to be bonded together permanently. Also, the "one flesh" relationship that results from the safety of this stability refers not only to sexual intimacy, but also to a transparent and nonthreatening intimacy in every other area of the relationship. This is the kind of openness depicted in the phrase "naked and not ashamed." Adam and Eve's unguarded physical openness reflected a wonderful spiritual, mental, and emotional freeness as well.

Ideally, that's marriage: two people living in close communion and harmony with God and one another. But then Adam and Eve sinned, and that beautiful ideal was badly damaged. Since then all marriages have struggled to experience close communion and harmony.

To find out how we can repair the damage sin has caused and remodel our marriages according to God's design, let's turn to Proverbs 24.

Proverbs 24:3–4

For many, the solution to a run-down marriage is to buy more things or to have children and make them the glue that holds the marriage together. For others the solution is even to change mates. But Solomon tells us that a strong marriage is not built on any of these shifting foundations, but on the bedrock of wisdom, understanding, and knowledge.

> By wisdom a house is built,
> And by understanding it is established;
> And by knowledge the rooms are filled
> With all precious and pleasant riches.
> (Prov. 24:3–4)

Notice the three verbs that are used: *built, established,* and *filled.* They're words that, on close inspection, describe the action of building and even remodeling a home.

Take the word *built,* for example. In Hebrew, it can mean to restore or rebuild something so that it flourishes. It's the same word used in Genesis 2 to describe how God rebuilt the rib taken from Adam's chest to form Eve. The hope we can draw out of this verse is that by wisdom even a home that may have fallen into disrepair can be restored to a flourishing state.

The second verb, *established*, means "to set in order, to place in an erect or upright position." By understanding, the home is set in order, made right, stabilized on the right footing.

Third, the verb *filled* means "overflowing." It's the idea of knowledge bringing fulfillment and abundant satisfaction to every room.

Put all three together and it's clear that it is possible for poorly designed and constructed marriages to be restored and made to flourish; to be set right and stabilized; and to be overflowing with precious and pleasant riches.[1]

To achieve such a radical renovation of our marriages, Solomon says we need three essential tools. First, *wisdom*—seeing with discernment. The term stresses accuracy, being able to see below the surface of things. It also includes the ability to look at self, others, and situations with a broader, more godly perspective.

Second, *understanding*—responding with insight. The Hebrew word suggests the idea of sifting out situations in order to gain full awareness for a proper response. In other words, understanding enables us to see beyond life's surface irritations with a depth of insight that brings order into a home.

And third, *knowledge*—learning with perception. This involves having a teachable spirit, a willingness to hear and to learn.

Equipped with these tools, we can construct marriages where close companionship and harmony with God and one another flourish. But how do we obtain wisdom, understanding, and knowledge? Where will we find them? Only one place. Turn to Proverbs 2:6.

> For the Lord gives wisdom;
> From His mouth come knowledge and understanding.

Only the Father can provide us with the tools we need. Certainly we're responsible for learning to use them skillfully, but they are, first of all, gifts from Him. This means that the Lord must be the cornerstone of the home. Without Him, Solomon reminds us in Psalm 127, our labor is futile.

> Unless the Lord builds the house,
> They labor in vain who build it;

1. Those riches, however, "have nothing to do with tangible possessions—but rather the essential things that make life full and meaningful. Things like positive attitudes, good relationships, pleasant memories, mutual respect, depth of character. The things that cannot be destroyed even though your home may burn to the ground." Charles R. Swindoll, *Strike the Original Match* (Portland, Oreg.: Multnomah Press, 1980), p. 23.

Unless the Lord guards the city,
The watchman keeps awake in vain.
(v. 1)

For the home to function as God designed it, He must be pre-
eminent. When He is Lord . . .

- He brings the skill of wisdom so that we can see with a discernment that encourages restoration.

- He provides calm understanding so we can respond with insight
  and set things in order.

- He makes knowledge a reality so that valuable and lasting traits
  might fill every room.

Application for the Home

We've been hard at it since we began this lesson, so take a break
to catch your breath, and when you're ready, consider these last
three remodeling tips.

First, the time to start is *now.* Remodeling your marriage isn't
a project for when the kids come or after they're gone. The time
is now. The longer you put it off, the more costly the repairs will
become. Second, the method to follow is God's. Don't keep relying
on old patterns for marriage that you picked up in the past. Follow
His instructions instead. And third, the person to change is you,
not your mate.

Most of us don't have to imagine how dysfunctional a marriage
can be when it's built according to our design instead of God's—we
know it feels, oftentimes, as if the kitchen sink is in the middle of
the dining room.

Instead of rearranging the furniture, why not consult the Architect and rebuild a whole new relationship, one where you'll want
to spend the rest of your life!

 Living Insights STUDY ONE

Oh, to be a fly on the wall of a counselor's office . . .

"Hello, Mr. Duffy. Please, sit down. Now, what would you like
to talk about?"

"Well, it's about my marriage."

"Yes?"

"Well, she's got a lot of problems."

"She?"

"My wife, I mean. We all do, of course; but she, well, she's hopeless. Something's always wrong. Nothing I do ever pleases her."

"So you came here to try to fix your wife?"

"Yes. She's making my life miserable."

◆

Now imagine Mr. Duffy's wife coming in to talk about their marriage . . .

"Good morning, Mrs. Duffy. Please have a seat."

"Thank you."

"From your phone call, it sounded as if you feel there are some serious problems in your marriage."

"Yes, he is."

"He?"

"My husband. How am I supposed to live with someone who constantly retreats behind a wall of silence and won't talk with me? I feel like he hides behind his work to avoid facing the problems we're having."

"And what would some of those problems be?"

"Well, first of all, he . . ."

◆

Exaggerated? Perhaps. But not by much. Marriage counselors hear this kind of blaming all the time. Peel away the adult veneer from Mr. and Mrs. Duffy's counseling sessions and what you have are two angry and frightened children pointing fingers at each other, saying,

"She did it!"

"No, he did, it's all his fault."

"Is not."

"Is too!"

Who's at fault? Many of us are hurting in our marriages, and we feel angry, bitter, and we want somebody to blame. We want to be able to point at someone and say, "There! There's the bad guy. He's the one responsible for this mess. Get him!" But the fact is, there are usually no "good guys" and "bad guys" in marriages. Just two selfish, imperfect people who want desperately to be in close

7

communion with each other but who are also desperately afraid to admit their own faults.

Are you really serious about remodeling your marriage according to God's design? Then you must be willing to let God remodel *you*. You must stop the vicious cycles of blaming and trying to reconstruct your mate according to your specifications, and give God permission to build in your life. He's got a great set of plans for you. Are you ready to go to work?

If so, make that commitment to Him right now in prayer.

 Living Insights

As we contemplate remodeling, the first thing we should do is walk through our marriages and appraise the areas where we need the most work. Spend some time in quiet prayer and meditation, asking God for His help in identifying what attitudes and practices need to be renovated or replaced.

Are there some walls you've built up that need to be torn down? Have you nailed any doors shut that need opening? What particular sinful responses or habits are causing cracks in the foundation? As thoughts come to mind, use the space provided to write up your appraisal.

Appraisal

_____

_____

_____

_____

_____

_____

_____

_____

_____

Chapter 2

THE PROJECT:
LET'S CONSIDER THE COST

Colossians 3:1–3, 5, 8–10

It's bound to happen. You'll come out to go somewhere in your car, either dressed in your best clothes or in a hurry to get to an important meeting, and one of the tires will be flat. "What? It wasn't flat last night," you'll say to yourself incredulously. "How did this happen?"

As you search for the missing piece to the jack, your mind begins rounding up suspects to blame for this unbelievably inconvenient phenomenon. "The neighbor's boy? Naahh. A three-year-old couldn't do this. Still . . . wait! Mike, the phantom prankster himself. He'd do this—he's capable. I'll get him. I'll flatten his tire. No! I'll take them, all four, right off his truck. That'll be great! He'll never . . . no, no Mike's out of town. Who then? Hmmm. The neighbor's boy, had to be."

And on and on your mind will work until eventually the mystery is solved and the real culprit is discovered—a slow leak. What appeared to be an overnight problem really wasn't. The tire had been going flat for some time; you just hadn't noticed it because the leak's effect was so subtle.

Many married couples have had a similar experience. They've gone along seemingly just fine for mile after mile, well past the ten-, twenty-, even thirty-year anniversary mark. Then suddenly one partner wakes up to find that the other has left, never to come back. Blowout? No. As Allan Petersen explains,

> Marriage is not wrecked by a blowout but rather by
> a slow leak—continued negligence and inattention.[1]

All too often, pastors and counselors hear the tragic words, "I had no idea she felt that way" or, "I never knew there was a problem." Slow leaks—they're not easy to detect, but they are just as deadly as a blowout.

---

1. J. Allan Petersen, ed., *The Marriage Affair* (Wheaton, Ill.: Tyndale House Publishers, 1971), p. 126.

Today we want to examine how to stop slow leaks from letting the air out of our marriages. What repairs can we make that will restore our relationships? In a word, the answer is *change*. It is the best patch we can apply, and it is also the most costly.

Change comes at a premium because it isn't easy for any of us. It's not in our nature to want to admit our faults or give up being selfish. And, too, change is costly because it is usually painful. Someone once said that the hardest two things to do in life are (1) to give up something old and (2) to take on something new. That's change, the true cost of remodeling a marriage.

Common Resistance against Restoring a Home

Because none of us enjoys paying the painful price connected with change, our natural tendency is to avoid patching the slow leaks in our marriages. Three methods people often use to avoid dealing with problems look something like this:

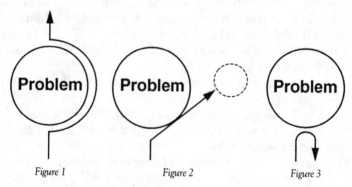

Figure 1   Figure 2   Figure 3

1. We Go around the Problem

Going around the problem is the response many couples perfect early on in marriage. Instead of working through a problem, they simply tiptoe past it, saying to themselves things like, "This issue really doesn't matter. What matters is raising the children." Or, "I don't want to rock the boat, so I'll just grin and bear it." Or, "I tried bringing this up before, and it didn't work. So why bother again?"

Still others attempt to sidestep problems by losing themselves in activities, organizations, and causes outside their home. And if the problem still stands in their way? They can always step around it with something like, "Well, at least we're doing better than the Joneses. Besides, nobody's perfect. Why worry?"

2. We Go Aside, Glance Off to a Phantom Problem

The second circle illustrates a more sophisticated method for avoiding problems. Here one or both spouses glance off the real issue and focus instead on a make-believe or "phantom" problem.

For example, a couple senses a growing irritation between them; but instead of facing it, they ricochet into thoughts like, "This isn't the same person I married. We're mismatched, that's our real problem. . . . Our real problem is that our love is dead. We need a divorce. We're just making things worse by staying together."

Others, in going beside the real problem, create even more trouble with such thoughts as, "What we really need are children to make this marriage work," or "more money" or "nicer things" or "more activities."

3. We Go Back, Claiming That It Is Impossible

A third reaction is the cop-out, "I'm too old and set in my ways to change. It's my nature to be hot-tempered. That's just the way I am. You can't teach an old dog new tricks; it's impossible. So don't even bother to try."

None of these three responses patch the problem. Instead, they allow the marital "leak" to remain intact and force us to adapt to and be subdued by it. The harder we try to deny a problem by going around, beside, or away from it, the more it will slowly deflate the love and enjoyment in our marriages, leaving them completely, painfully flat.

There is a way, however, to keep slow leaks from developing in our marriages, as illustrated in this next diagram.

Figure 4

4. We Go through the Problem, Working It Out

The only way to prevent a problem from becoming a slow leak is to work through it. And that means being committed to *change*. It's expensive; but the rewards, as those who have risked the pain already know, are well worth it.

For help in understanding what costly changes are needed to work through problems in our marriages, let's turn to Colossians 3.

Costly Responses That Restore a Home

The apostle Paul begins his counsel by issuing an important command—keep seeking!

> If then you have been raised up with Christ, keep seeking the things above, where Christ is, seated at the right hand of God. (Col. 3:1)

Is it your life's goal to keep seeking the things above? A seeking attitude is a costly one. It pushes us to pursue Christ through problems, even when the pain is intense and we'd like to settle for something less than His best. But how, exactly, do we cultivate this kind of attitude? What process should we pursue? The answer is revealed in verse 2.

> Set your mind on the things above, not on the things that are on earth.

Paul directs us to the realm of the mind. Seeking begins in setting our minds on the things of Christ. We're to concentrate on the eternal, as the Apostle explained to the Philippians,

> Finally, brethren, whatever is true, whatever is honorable, whatever is right, whatever is pure, whatever is lovely, whatever is of good repute, if there is any excellence and if anything worthy of praise, let your mind dwell on these things. (4:8)

Why?

> For you have died and your life is hidden with Christ in God. (Col. 3:3)

The selfish ego part of us has died—it's been crucified with Christ. And we're to count ourselves as dead to sin but alive to Christ (Rom. 6:11). What does that mean for everyday living? Paul explained it this way in his letter to the Romans.

> And do not go on presenting the members of your
> body to sin as instruments of unrighteousness; but
> present yourselves to God as those alive from the
> dead, and your members as instruments of righteous-
> ness to God. (6:13)

This is how, on a practical, moment-by-moment level, we demonstrate the truth that our lives are hidden in Christ. Paul gets
even more specific back in our Colossians passage.

> Therefore consider the members of your earthly
> body as dead to immorality, impurity, passion, evil
> desire, and greed, which amounts to idolatry. . . .
> But now you also, put them all aside: anger, wrath,
> malice, slander, and abusive speech from your mouth.
> Do not lie to one another, since you laid aside the
> old self with its evil practices. (3:5, 8–10)

To bring Paul's counsel closer to home, let's translate it into
four responses that help restore a marriage.

1. *Dig in.* Take an honest look at who you really are in your
home. What are you like to live with? What areas need changing?
Write them down if it will help. Dig in to discover what's inside you.

2. *Give up.* Stop fighting for your rights. Stop defending your
wrong behavior. Instead, listen to what your mate or your children
have to say about the things that need changing. And when your
family is honest enough to tell you, don't argue and try to hit back
by pointing out all their weaknesses. Just listen. Give up those
things that are hurting others and yourself.

3. *Start over.* In Paul's words, "put on the new self" (3:10).
Confess your wrongs, accept forgiveness, and learn to walk in new-
ness of life patterned after Christ. Start over. And the next time
you blow it, start over again. And keep starting over no matter how
many times it takes.

4. *Carry through.* Like most of us, you've probably formed old
habits that have been puncturing the relationship for years, so you
can be sure no slipshod patch job is going to keep your marriage
from going flat. Keep changing; don't stop making an effort at it.
Sure, it will be work, probably the hardest work you will ever do.
But the old patterns can be replaced by God's grace. Carry through.

This same costly advice from Colossians 3 is summed up by the
apostle Paul in Ephesians 4. He writes:

That, in reference to your former manner of life, you lay aside the old self, which is being corrupted in accordance with the lusts of deceit, and that you be renewed in the spirit of your mind, and put on the new self, which in the likeness of God has been created in righteousness and holiness of the truth. (vv. 22–24)

Lay aside the old self—dig in, give up. Put on the new self—start over, carry through. That's change. For it to become permanent, we need to be both putting off the old and putting on the new. One without the other doesn't lead to permanent transformation.

Take lying, for example. When is a liar not a liar? When that person stops lying? No. That's only the putting-off part. Paul takes it a step further:

Therefore, laying aside falsehood, speak truth, each one of you, with his neighbor, for we are members of one another. (v. 25)

For people who have a problem with lying to truly change, they must not only put off telling lies, they must also put on telling the truth. This same principle is applied to the one who steals.

Let him who steals steal no longer; but rather let him labor, performing with his own hands what is good, in order that he may have something to share with him who has need. (v. 28)

From someone who takes to someone who gives. Now that's permanent, transforming change. The kind that we're capable of *if* we keep seeking Christ, who said, "If anyone wishes to come after Me, let him deny himself [dig in, give up], and take up his cross [start over], and follow Me [carry through]" (Matt. 16:24).

Uncommon Rewards of a Restored Home

Many of us come into marriage with misconceptions of what it will be like. We expect it to be a blissful state, a happily-ever-after union like the ones we've read about in books and seen on the silver screen.

Sooner or later, however, those illusions get shattered by the flesh-and-blood realities of what it's like when two sinful and selfish people live together under one roof. That's no fairy tale. The pain is real. But the joys can also be real, if we're willing to pay the cost of remodeling our marriages according to God's design, if we're willing to change.

A restored home is its own reward, but there's more. Think of the children in that home. Think of the reward of seeing them learn how to dig in, give up, start over, and carry through. Think of the needless pain that can be avoided if they enter their own marriages already skilled at using the tools of wisdom, understanding, and knowledge that we discussed in our last lesson.

Change is expensive, but the rewards of a restored home far outweigh the cost. How much are you willing to pay to patch the leaks in your marriage?

 ## Living Insights STUDY ONE

What is it like to be married to you? Would you be afraid to give your spouse ten minutes of uninterrupted time to tell you?

Yes, most of us would. It's risky. It means opening ourselves up to hear about slow leaks we didn't even know existed, much less know we had caused. And that could hurt.

But hurt how, why? Because it wounds our pride to admit that we've made mistakes? Or because we would feel genuinely grieved about the way we've failed to love our spouses? Something to think about. Especially if you're interested in pursuing this idea of giving your mate ten minutes. It's a great way to patch slow leaks, but not if your goal in marriage is self-protection.

For those of you willing to dig in, give up, start over, and carry through toward the goal of loving your spouse more deeply, take a moment now to pencil in a time and place you think would be most convenient for him or her to have ten uninterrupted minutes with you.

Date: _____ Time: _____ Place: _____

The rules for this exercise are simple. (1) Let your spouse know ahead of time what you're planning and why so that he or she can have time to think through the question. (2) Once you've asked the question, "What is it like living with me?" your only job is to listen. That's ten minutes when you don't say a thing except to ask for further clarification on anything you don't understand. Only clarification, though; no comments. Remember, the goal here is not to refute, argue, or win, but to listen for the slow leaks that you may be causing.

Afterwards, use the next Living Insight to work your way through the four steps outlined in the lesson—and see if you can patch that leak!

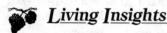 **Living Insights**

During that ten-minute time, you probably heard at least one slow leak that needs patching. Don't allow yourself to go around this problem or beside or away from it. Go straight at it by digging right in.

Dig In

In what area is there a need for change? Be specific. Pray for God's guidance. Seek outside help if you feel it could help clarify what the problem is. When you think you understand it, write it down.

_____

_____

_____

Give Up

What is it that I need to put off? Is there a specific attitude or action that you can identify? Putting off a sinful behavior is great, but we must do more than simply change our actions. We must also change our thinking. Why do you do this particular thing? What's your motivation? Get to the root of this problem by asking these kinds of questions. See if you can uncover the wrong thinking that prompts you to act in this way. Again, if you need help, seek out a trusted friend, pastor, or counselor for help.

_____

_____

_____

_____

_____

Start Over

What must be put on? You've identified a way of thinking and living that needs to be put off. Now let's focus on what must be put on in its place. Can you think of any particular Scripture that might help renew your thinking in a more holy, healthy pattern? Once you've identified the thinking that must be renewed (see Rom. 12:1–2), brainstorm new habits that need to be put into practice.

_____

_____

_____

_____

_____

Carry Through

Make this a pattern. Old patterns that have been ingrained in us since childhood don't change easily or overnight. Don't heap guilt on yourself if you fail in this endeavor not more than five minutes after you begin. Jesus still loves you. He knows your weaknesses and will patiently, lovingly continue to work with you. Just don't give up. Keep trusting in Him for His strength. He wants you to change, to patch that leak. And by His grace, you will!

Chapter 3

LET'S REPAIR
THE FOUNDATION

Genesis 2:18–25

J une and Ward Cleaver. Who can forget America's most perfect
couple?

"Honey, I'm home!" Ward says.

"Oh, hi, dear." June smiles as she comes walking out of her spotless kitchen wearing the usual
aproned dress, high heels, pearls, perfect makeup,
and a perky little smile. "How was your day?"

"Just fine, dear. Where are the boys?"

"Wally and Eddie went down to Mrs. Simpson's
to plant gardenias. They cut down every one she
had yesterday while mowing her yard. And the
Beaver is upstairs studying his homework."

Ah, the perfect couple. The model marriage. Television's grown-
up version of Ken and Barbie. Oh, sure, they had problems; but
that was always because of one of the boys, never because June and
Ward weren't getting along. You never saw Ward lose it and start
yelling at June in front of Wally and the Beaver. And June never
came out of the kitchen in hysterics, weeping and threatening to

leave if Ward didn't stop spending money they didn't have. No, everything between those two was always nice and neat and tidy. Ideal.

In real marriages, however, things are rarely nice, neat, and tidy. Most couples would love it if they could get along as effortlessly as June and Ward did. But the truth is, no couple does. Idyllic relationships like that don't exist in this fallen world. At best, some couples may be wonderfully adjusted and harmonious, but their marriages still aren't ideal.

Only one couple throughout all of history has ever enjoyed an ideal marriage. It wasn't Abraham and Sarah, or Noah and his wife, or even Joseph and Mary. That one fortunate couple who experienced the ideal, for a brief time, was Adam and Eve. Let's turn to Genesis 2 and note why.

Clarification: One "Ideal" Marriage

Four ingredients went into making Adam and Eve's marriage ideal. First, *God made a perfect fit* (Gen. 2:18–22a). Eve was custom-built from one of Adam's own ribs. She was faultlessly fitted for him. He didn't have to guess if she was the right one for him—when God makes something ideally suited for you, it's perfect.

Second, *God brought them together* (v. 22b). Adam didn't have to go through any difficult process to find a mate. Eve was a special delivery from God right to his front doorstep!

Third, *Eve was originally a part of Adam* (v. 23). No adjustments or adaptations had to be made between this first couple. Neither one had any bad habits or extra baggage from different families that needed to be discarded. They were literally of the same flesh and bone. A perfect match.

And fourth, *they were totally innocent.* Adam and Eve's relationship and world started out sinlessly. They weren't trying to hide anything because there wasn't anything to hide. Neither of them knew anything about guilt or shame. They only knew the fulfilling, exhilarating oneness of an ideal marriage.

Since the day that first couple sinned, however (see Gen. 3), no marriage has ever been ideal. Ideal relationships exist only in our minds, not in reality. Yet many of us actually enter into marriage with the romantic notion that it will be ideal. We place incredible demands on our spouses to be perfect mates who will meet all our needs. Sooner or later, though, reality forces us to see that Prince Charming has chinks in his armor and Sleeping Beauty wakes up on the wrong side of the bed. And the marriage that we thought would be so effortless becomes a daily struggle.

What can we do?

We can fight reality and continue to demand the ideal from our spouses . . . or we can look to the only One who is ideal and rebuild our marriages according to His realistic principles.

Exposition: Four Biblical Principles

Following Adam's first awestruck response to Eve, the Lord laid down four truths to serve as a solid foundation for all marriages.

> For this cause a man shall leave his father and his mother, and shall cleave to his wife; and they shall become one flesh. And the man and his wife were both naked and were not ashamed. (2:24–25)

The Lord's four principles are *severance, permanence, acceptance,* and *intimacy.* Let's dig in to the first three now and save the fourth for a later chapter where we will explore it more fully.

Severance

> For this cause a man shall leave his father and his mother. (v. 24a)

The first step in creating a new union with our spouses is the dissolving of the old one with our parents. We're to "leave," which in Hebrew carries the idea of departing, loosing oneself, finding freedom from something.

The Lord used a strong term here, but not a harsh one. In separating ourselves from our parents and becoming physically, mentally, and emotionally independent, there isn't to be any bitterness. We're not to forsake them as if they were the enemy. Nothing like that is being suggested here. Nor is God saying that we should ignore their counsel as if there is nothing more they can teach us. On the contrary, they have a great deal of wisdom of which we would be smart to avail ourselves. So listen to their advice. Then make your own decisions—and be responsible for them.

From a parent's perspective, severing means training a child so that he or she can become independent in a healthy, natural, flowing fashion. And one of the evidences of good training is a child's ability to make wise decisions. We can encourage this by not waiting to release our children until they're grown, but by slowly releasing the reins and giving them more and more responsibilities as they mature physically, mentally, emotionally, and spiritually.

For those of us who are already married, remember this practical tip: Leaving means that you don't continually quote Mom or compare your spouse with Dad. "Well, honey, Mom says you should always do the Thanksgiving turkey in a paper bag." Or, "Dad never would have done it like that." Or, "That's good, dear, but you should have seen the way Mom always did that." Bringing the parents into the new home this way can create all kinds of problems. God says leave. Separate yourselves from your parents by developing your own ways of doing things that reflect your unique tastes and talents.

Permanence

And [he] shall cleave to his wife. (v. 24b)

The second principle for us to discover is found in the word *cleave*. In Hebrew, it means to cling, to glue, to keep close, and to remain constant. Marriage is to be a permanent relationship. A secure, unbreakable bond.

Many marriages today, however, are entered into with the idea that the couple can always call it quits if things don't work out the way they thought it would.

Something happens in a marriage when a husband or wife begins entertaining the thought of leaving. It's difficult to explain, but somehow a change occurs, a crack develops in the bond that holds the marriage together. If not repaired, that fissure grows each time the marriage faces stress; the bond eventually crumbles and the marriage is dissolved.

Jesus said, "What therefore God has joined together, let no man separate" (Matt. 19:6b). So the question we must ask ourselves during difficult times is not, How can I get out of my marriage? but, How can I make it better? That's marriage with a permanent attitude.

Acceptance

And they [the husband and wife] shall become one
flesh. (v. 24c)

The third principle differs from the previous two in that they were more decisions of the mind. Becoming one flesh, however, represents involvement—the practical working out of the union formed on the wedding day. It's a process that takes time. And the major attitude needed to foster this in a marriage is acceptance.

Communicating that acceptance involves such thoughts and feelings as, "You are the one God gave me, and I accept you exactly as you are. You don't have to perform to earn my love or support. Just like me, you are imperfect; but that doesn't make me wish we weren't husband and wife. I promise to give myself to you as an encouragement and to be honest with you."

One insightful article in *Eternity* magazine defined acceptance this way.

> It means you are valuable just as you are. It allows you to be the *real* you. You aren't forced into someone else's idea of who you really are. It means your ideas are taken seriously since they reflect you. You can talk about how you feel inside and why you feel that way—and someone really cares.
>
> Acceptance means you can try out your ideas without being shot down. You can even express heretical thoughts and discuss them with intelligent questioning. You feel safe. No one will pronounce judgment on you, even though they don't agree with you. It doesn't mean you will never be corrected or shown to be wrong; it simply means it is safe to be *you* and no one will destroy *you* out of prejudice.[1]

This is the kind of unconditional love that enables two people to become one flesh. There's no belittling, no tearing down with sarcasm, only building up through constant affirmation and affection.

Application: Two Timely Reminders

Since all husbands and wives struggle with marriages that are less than ideal, it might be helpful to remember that God doesn't expect perfection. Yet even though an *ideal* marriage may not be possible, a *good* marriage is. And the way to repair our marriages, to make them healthy and honoring to God, is by application—that's what He expects.

We need to apply the realistic instructions we've studied today, not just file them away in a notebook. More often than not, if our

1. Gladys M. Hunt, "That's No Generation Gap!" *Eternity,* October 1969, p. 15.

marriages are getting worse, it's not because the truth is flawed; rather, our appropriation of the truth is lacking.

Also, even though you may apply these truths in your marriage by yourself, it's better if you can put them into practice with your spouse. It will make the process more effective and much sweeter as well.

 ### *Living Insights* STUDY ONE

St. John of the Cross once wrote, "At the evening of our day, we shall be judged by our loving." That "evening" is the culmination of all our choices and judgments, actions and apathies, things spoken and unspoken which have shaped our lives and reflect the depth or lack of love within us.

How well are you loving your spouse? Think about your choices and judgments, actions and apathies, things spoken and unspoken yesterday. Were they bathed in an accepting, unconditional kind of love? Use the following space to take inventory of the depth or lack of acceptance you demonstrated yesterday.

_____

_____

_____

_____

_____

_____

_____

_____

Some of us (dare I say most?) may be shocked at the lack of positive things we could honestly find to put down. The paltry ways many of us love our spouses actually reflects a real poverty in the way we feel loved. So how can we improve the way we love our mates? Demand that they love us better so that we'll love them better back? Of course not. But what then?

Many might answer, "Simply make a commitment to try harder to love my spouse." But that won't work either. How can we try harder to give something we don't have?

The only way we can nurture the loving acceptance we're starving for is by going to the One who is love Himself. Remember the apostle John's insight, "We love, because He first loved us" (1 John 4:19)? Have you lost touch with God's love for you? Have all the activities of life deadened that deep, freeing sense of being totally loved and accepted by Him? When's the last time you were overwhelmed by that love?

For many of us, what we need to hear is not that we should be loving our spouses better. That only adds to our guilt. What we really need to hear afresh is how deeply God loves us. We need to feel that incredible love, to experience it in a personal way. Have you allowed yourself to slow down lately, long enough for Him to hold you and love you?

Let Him wrap His arms around you right now. Be still. Meditate on His lovingkindness toward you. Listen.

> What then shall we say to these things? If God is for us, who is against us? He who did not spare His own Son, but delivered Him up for us all, how will He not also with Him freely give us all things? Who will bring a charge against God's elect? God is the one who justifies; who is the one who condemns? Christ Jesus is He who died, yes rather who was raised, who is at the right hand of God, who also intercedes for us. Who shall separate us from the love of Christ? Shall tribulation, or distress, or persecution, or famine, or nakedness, or peril, or sword? Just as it is written,
>
>> "For Thy sake we are being put to death all day long;
>> We were considered as sheep to be slaughtered."
>
> But in all these things we overwhelmingly conquer through Him who loved us. For I am convinced that neither death, nor life, nor angels, nor principalities, nor things present, nor things to come, nor powers, nor height, nor depth, nor any other created

thing, shall be able to separate us from the love of God, which is in Christ Jesus our Lord. (Rom. 8:31–39)

Allow God to love you. Put everything away and just sit in His lap. For only when we yield to His amazing love will we be capable of loving our spouses well.

 ## Living Insights

Not everyone's spouse will want to repair their marriage according to God's design. But for those of you whose mate is willing, set aside some time to talk through this Living Insight together.

As we saw from our lesson, severance, permanence, and acceptance are foundational principles to marriage. And yet most of us have probably never really sat down and talked about these with our spouses. So that's your assignment. Set aside a time and place where you can explore these principles with one another.[2]

Severance

Spend some time just talking about the severance process both of you have gone through with your parents. Explore one another's thoughts and feelings about severing from your parents by asking questions such as, "Was it a healthy process? Were there any hurts? Did you feel prepared to go out on your own as a responsible adult? Do you feel your parents have let you go? What do you wish would have been done differently?" and so forth.

Permanence

Take turns answering the first question before you go on to the second.

1. What are some of the things my spouse does for me or we do together that nurture the feeling of permanence in our marriage?

2. How can I make our bond feel more permanent?

---

2. Rather than sit at the kitchen table and do this, why not go to your favorite park or scenic spot? Maybe even go for a long walk.

Acceptance

Finally, explore this principle by asking each other the following questions. Let them be a catalyst to take you as deep into this subject as you know how to go.

1. Growing up, did you feel accepted in your family for who you were—warts and all? Or did you have to perform in order to earn your parents' approval?

2. Today, do you still feel as if you have to perform to be accepted? Is your love toward your spouse dependent on his or her performance?

3. What are some ways that both of you can foster a deeper sense of acceptance in the love between you?

Chapter 4

In Defense of Monogamy

Selected Scripture

Some time ago, an actor known for his romantic roles in movies was asked by a television talk show host, "What makes a great lover?" To the surprise of the host and many in the audience, he said, "A great lover is someone who can satisfy one woman all her life long; and who can be satisfied by one woman all his life long. A great lover is not someone who goes from woman to woman. Any dog can do that!"

In today's dog-eat-dog world, unfortunately, it is the instincts of the dog that are being promoted and praised among people. We're just animals too, right? So why not live by instinct and find gratification with whomever, whenever? Fidelity, commitment, trust? That's Victorian stuff. Nobody listens to that anymore. Marriage to one partner for life is ancient history!

This is what we hear every day over the radio, in movies, magazines, on television, and in schools across the country. Humankind has been stripped of the dignity bestowed on it by the Creator and reduced to being products of evolution encouraged to mate and move on like stray dogs. It's harsh, but such is the reality that we live in.

It's time we freed ourselves from the leash of that miserable philosophy. We're not dogs, nor can we live like them without causing incredible damage and suffering to ourselves and others— even for generations down the line.

In this lesson, we want to give you a positive message and reminder of God's design for healthy marriages: *monogamy.*

Some Initial Terms to Clarify

Let's begin our study by defining monogamy along with two other important words related to this subject.

Monogamy: In Greek, two terms are used to make up this one word—*monos,* meaning "once" or "only," and *gamos,* meaning "marriage, once married." It can be translated one of two ways: "married

This message was not a part of the original series but is compatible with it.

to one person throughout life" or "married to one person at a time." Essentially, it signifies a one-man, one-woman relationship.

Commitment: This word gets tossed around a lot, especially in Christian circles, but rarely is it explained. Commitment means a stated trust, a pledged agreement. As believers, we pledge to both God and our spouses to keep our vows in marriage.

Accountability: Another word often used but seldom defined is *accountability,* which means to answer, explain, or give reasons for one's actions. We should note that Christians have the added obligation of answering to the Lord as well as to their spouse.

A Study of the Monogamy-Polygamy Conflict

When understood and applied correctly, these three words are at the heart of God's original design for the marriage relationship. But tragically, that plan was thrown away and another was substituted— one that has sent shock waves of destruction through history to this present day. Let's take a brief tour through the Scriptures to see where and how things went wrong.

Survey of Scripture

As you may remember from our earlier studies, when God brought Adam and Eve together He immediately established the timeless principle of monogamy.

> For this cause a man shall leave his father and his mother, and shall cleave to his wife; and they shall become one flesh. (Gen. 2:24)

In Genesis 4:19, however, only two chapters later, Scripture records the first instance of someone breaking that command. Not surprisingly, it is one of Cain's descendants (vv. 16–18).

> And Lamech took to himself two wives: the name of the one was Adah, and the name of the other, Zillah. (v. 19)

Even after the Flood, polygamy was still an accepted practice, as we see in the lives of Jacob and Esau (chaps. 26, 29). So it isn't surprising that as Israel's history continues, we find Moses reiterating a regulation for untangling problems created by polygamy.

> "If a man has two wives, the one loved and the other unloved, and both the loved and the unloved

have borne him sons, if the first-born son belongs to the unloved, then it shall be in the day he wills what he has to his sons, he cannot make the son of the loved the first-born before the son of the un-loved, who is the first-born. But he shall acknowl-edge the first-born, the son of the unloved, by giving him a double portion of all that he has, for he is the beginning of his strength; to him belongs the right of the first-born." (Deut. 21:15–17)

Notice how matter-of-factly Moses addresses this issue. He's not even shocked that polygamy exists. It was so widespread by then that it became necessary to institute laws to govern it.

Another case of polygamy is found in 1 Samuel 1.

Now there was a certain man from Ramathaim-zophim from the hill country of Ephraim, and his name was Elkanah. . . . And he had two wives: the name of one was Hannah and the name of the other Peninnah. (vv. 1–2a)

Again, notice how straightforwardly this sin is mentioned. It's almost as if polygamy were the rule rather than the exception. Obedience to God's original command for monogamy, even among those who worshiped the Lord, had eroded greatly. Perhaps more than any other, Solomon epitomizes the problem with his seven hundred wives and three hundred concubines (see 1 Kings 11:1–3)!

As we turn to the New Testament, however, we'll find that God's original design of monogamy is consistently affirmed. In Matthew 19, for example, the Pharisees, hoping to embroil Jesus in a debate about divorce, instead get a lesson on monogamy.

And some Pharisees came to [Jesus], testing Him, and saying, "Is it lawful for a man to divorce his wife for any cause at all?" And He answered and said, "Have you not read, that He who created them from the beginning made them male and female, and said, 'For this cause a man shall leave his father and mother, and shall cleave to his wife; and the two shall be-come one flesh'? Consequently they are no longer two, but one flesh. What therefore God has joined together, let no man separate." (vv. 3–6)

Monogamy is also upheld by the apostle Paul, who wrote more about marriage than anyone else in the Scriptures. Take 1 Corinthians 7, for example. In that one chapter alone he deals with a whole range of marital issues, such as singleness, marriage, desertion, divorce, and remarriage. Polygamy, however, is never mentioned. It's conspicuously absent. In fact, as you read through Paul's counsel, what is prominent is his belief in and endorsement of monogamous relationships: "Let each man have his own wife, and let each woman have her own husband" (v. 2).

In a more specific way, he mentions monogamy twice in his lists of qualifications for an overseer and deacon in 1 Timothy 3.

> It is a trustworthy statement: if any man aspires to the office of overseer, it is a fine work he desires to do. An overseer, then, must be above reproach, the husband of one wife, temperate, prudent, respectable, hospitable, able to teach. . . . Let deacons be husbands of only one wife, and good managers of their children and their own households. (vv. 1–2, 12)

Conclusions to Consider

From this sampling of Old and New Testament passages, we can draw a couple of important conclusions concerning monogamy and polygamy.

First, *the Bible records the truth about polygamy, but it does not justify it.* The fact that God's Word is inerrant guarantees that what it reports is true. But not everything reported is what the Bible teaches. Take, for example, Satan's comment to Eve, "You surely shall not die!" (Gen. 3:4). It's true that Satan said that, but what Satan said was not true. In the same way, even though polygamy is reported in the Bible, we know with certainty that the Bible teaches monogamy.

Second, *while polygamy may not be directly condemned, its evil effects are clearly revealed.* One of the most tragic examples of this comes from the life of David. Among his eight wives was a woman named Maacah, who bore him a son named Absalom and a beautiful daughter named Tamar. Now Amnon, son from one of David's other wives, lusted after Tamar. Feigning an illness to get Tamar in his room, he then forced himself on her. Absalom found out about the rape and later murdered his half-brother Amnon.

Consider commentator Alexander Whyte's candid description of the home situation in which Absalom, Tamar, Amnon, and

David's children grew up in because David ignored God's command for monogamy in marriage.

> Polygamy is just Greek for a dunghill. David trampled down the first and the best law of nature in his palace in Jerusalem, and for his trouble he spent all his after-days in a hell upon earth. David's palace was a perfect pandemonium of suspicion, and intrigue, and jealousy, and hatred—all breaking out, now into incest and now into murder. . . .
>
> A little ring of jealous and scheming parasites, all hateful and hating one another, collected round each one of David's wives. And it was in one of the worst of those wicked little rings that Absalom grew up and got his education.[1]

When you consider the consequences of David's polygamous relationships, it's easy to understand why God designed marriage to be a one-man, one-woman union involving commitment and accountability. Those aren't options for a healthy marriage; they're essentials. And all three are beautifully woven together in the Jewish term for marriage—*kiddushin*.

> *Kiddushin* means *sanctification* or *consecration*. It was used to describe something which was dedicated to God as his exclusive and peculiar possession. Anything totally surrendered to God was *kiddushin*. This meant that in marriage the husband was consecrated to the wife, and the wife to the husband. The one became the exclusive possession of the other, as much as an offering became the exclusive possession of God. That is what Jesus meant when He said that for the sake of marriage a man would leave his father and his mother and cleave to his wife; and that is what He meant when He said that man and wife became so totally one that they could be called one flesh. That was God's ideal of marriage.[2]

1. Alexander Whyte, *Bible Characters* (London, England: Oliphants, 1952), vol. 1, p. 309.

2. William Barclay, *The Gospel of Matthew*, vol. 2, rev. ed., The Daily Study Bible Series (Philadelphia, Pa.: Westminster Press, 1975), pp. 202–3.

Is your marriage *kiddushin?* Have you dedicated it to God as His exclusive possession? Are you absolutely given and totally surrendered to remodeling your marriage according to His design? Then dedicate and consecrate yourself to your mate, and, "forsaking all others, keep thee only unto [your mate], so long as ye both shall live."[3]

Say, "I will!"

 ## *Living Insights* STUDY ONE

No one thinks he needs hedges until it's too late.[4]

John didn't. "We're just good friends," he told himself. "Sue is a good business associate, that's all. I respect her. Anything wrong with that?" No. About eight months later, however, it was Sue who was waking up in bed beside John, and not his wife.

Why? Because John and Sue were immoral reprobates? Not at all. They started out, in fact, a lot like many of us. Responsible, committed Christians, with no thought or intention of ever cheating on their spouse.

Impossible, some of you think? Careful, that's what John and Sue thought. That's why, when they were together, neither of them put up any hedges to protect against an affair developing. It all started out innocently enough; but then slowly, imperceptibly, they began to depend on each other emotionally. They shared private plans and ambitions, justified lunches together and exchanged physical touches that were "brotherly, sisterly." The two liked each other, became special to each other, and eventually became enamored with each other. Then the inevitable happened.[5]

Regardless of how committed we are to Christ and our marriages, we all need hedges to protect ourselves from naively allowing a relationship like John and Sue's to develop in our lives. In his book *Hedges*, Jerry Jenkins candidly shares the hedges he has developed to protect himself and his marriage. Here are just a few:

3. *Minister's Manual* (Bradley, Ill.: Evangelical Church Alliance, 1982), p. 55.

4. Jerry B. Jenkins, *Hedges* (Brentwood, Tenn.: Wolgemuth and Hyatt, Publishers, 1989), p. 5.

5. Based on a story told in *Hedges*, by Jerry Jenkins, pp. 7–14.

Hedge No. 1—Whenever I need to meet or dine or travel with an unrelated woman, I make it a three-some. Should an unavoidable last-minute complication make this impossible, my wife hears it from me first. . . .

Hedge No. 2—I am careful about touching. While I might shake hands or squeeze an arm or a shoulder in greeting, I embrace only dear friends or relatives, and only in front of others. . . .

Hedge No. 6—From the time I get home from work until the children go to bed, I do no writing or office work. This gives me lots of time with the family and for my wife and me to continue to court and date.[6]

Now that we have an idea of what a hedge looks like, let's plant some around our own marriages in the next Living Insight.

🍇 Living Insights   STUDY TWO

Take some time now with your spouse to brainstorm the kinds of hedges you both want to protect your marriage.

1. _____

_____

2. _____

_____

3. _____

_____

4. _____

_____

5. _____

_____

6. Jenkins, *Hedges*, pp. 75, 85, 123.

Chapter 5

BRICKS THAT BUILD A MARRIAGE

1 Peter 3:1–9

Four-year-old Suzie had just been told the story
of "Snow White" for the first time in her life. She
could hardly wait to get home from nursery school
to tell her mommy. With wide-eyed excitement, she
retold the fairy tale to her mother that afternoon.
After relating how Prince Charming had arrived on
his beautiful white horse and kissed Snow White
back to life, Suzie asked loudly:

"And do you know what happened then?"

"Yes," said her mom, "they lived happily ever
after."

"No," responded Suzie, with a frown, ". . . they
got married."[1]

In her childlike innocence, Suzie touched on the poignant truth
that getting married and living happily ever after are not necessarily synonymous.

The reason is perhaps best illustrated by another familiar childhood story, "The Three Little Pigs." Like the first two brothers,
many couples build their marriages out of straw and sticks, only to
have them collapse when adversity blows. The more solid, lasting,
and enjoyable marriages, however, are built out of the same material
the third brother used—bricks.

In our lesson today, the apostle Peter will be giving us the bricks
we need to build strong marriages, as well as the mortar necessary
to hold them together. But before we find out what these bricks
are, let's look at the plans we're to follow in using them, plans
revealed in Ephesians 5.

---

1. Charles R. Swindoll, *Strike the Original Match* (Portland, Oreg.: Multnomah Press, 1980),
p. 39.

Discovering the Pattern to Be Used

Speaking first to wives and then to husbands, the apostle Paul outlines the role for each and gives an analogy emphasizing their significance.

For the Wife

> Wives, be subject to your own husbands, as to the Lord. For the husband is the head of the wife, as Christ also is the head of the church, He Himself being the Savior of the body. But as the church is subject to Christ, so also the wives ought to be to their husbands in everything. . . . Let the wife see to it that she respect her husband. (Eph. 5:22–24, 33b)

Paul lays out God's plan for the wife with a command: "Wives, be subject to your own husbands," and then an analogy: "as to the Lord" (v. 22). The general pattern for the role of the wife is submission to the husband. If the wife were to ask God, "How shall I show my love to You in the role You have given me to fill?" God would answer, "My dear child, show it in the submission you have to your husband."

For the Husband

> Husbands, love your wives, just as Christ also loved the church and gave Himself up for her; that He might sanctify her, having cleansed her by the washing of water with the word, that He might present to Himself the church in all her glory, having no spot or wrinkle or any such thing; but that she should be holy and blameless. So husbands ought also to love their own wives as their own bodies. He who loves his own wife loves himself; for no one ever hated his own flesh, but nourishes and cherishes it, just as Christ also does the church, because we are members of His body. For this cause a man shall leave his father and mother, and shall cleave to his wife; and the two shall become one flesh. This mystery is great; but I am speaking with reference to Christ and the church. Nevertheless let each individual among you also love his own wife even as himself. (vv. 25–33a)

Again, Paul presents a command: "Husbands, love your wives," and then an analogy: "as Christ also loved the church and gave Himself up for her" (v. 25). The basic role for the husband is adoration. If the husband were to ask, "Lord, how shall I show my love to You in the role You've given me?" God would answer, "My son, the love you have for your wife shows Me and this world the kind of love you have for Me."

Implied in these verses concerning the husband's and wife's roles are two searching questions. As the wife models her role according to the pattern of submission, she is faced with the question, Do I love my husband enough to *live* for him? And for the man, as he fulfills the role of adoration as a husband, he is faced with the question, Do I love my wife enough to *die* for her?

Today, neither question is a popular one. The concepts of submission and adoration are highly criticized and rejected as being too confining, enslaving, and demanding. But, inevitably, those who feel that way have failed to understand the biblical picture of subjection and adoration. Nowhere does God's pattern for marriage encourage either spouse to demean or take advantage of the other. Quite the opposite. When lived out rightly, a wonderful fulfillment and freedom is possible for the husband and wife that is rarely experienced anywhere else.

Now that we have seen the general pattern for building or rebuilding our marriages, we must choose the right bricks for the project. And here to help us with our selection is the apostle Peter.

Choosing the Bricks That Are Essential

In the first six verses of 1 Peter 3, the Apostle hands wives four bricks essential to building a strong marriage.

You Wives . . .

The first brick is titled *actions.*

> In the same way, you wives, be submissive to your own husbands so that even if any of them are disobedient to the word, they may be won without a word by the behavior of their wives, as they observe your chaste and respectful behavior. (vv. 1–2)

The tendency for many is to read this and say, "Sure, I'll be happy to be that kind of wife—IF—he's the right kind of husband." But that misses a major point of the passage. Peter is writing here with the wrong kind of husband in mind—"even if any of them are disobedient" (v. 1).

Instead of hitting these kinds of husbands with a brick, wives are to win them back to the Lord by demonstrating the solid brick of "chaste and respectful behavior." Nagging, shaming, preaching—these only alienate the man and worsen the situation. But the powerful witness of a wife's submissive behavior, Peter says, will attract the husband's attention and draw him back.

To emphasize this, the Apostle uses a Greek term for *observe* that means "to peer intently at an athletic event." Make no mistake about it, even though a husband may be stubborn and rebellious toward the Lord, he still studies and watches his wife intently when she lets her faith speak through her godly behavior.

The second brick is labeled *adornment.*

> And let not your adornment be merely external—
> braiding the hair, and wearing gold jewelry, or put-
> ting on dresses. (v. 3)

Notice the words "merely external." Peter isn't attacking or criticizing externals such as hairstyles and clothing. He's not saying, "Ignore the way you look!" Rather, he is telling wives not to go overboard in their preoccupation with external appearance. The adornment of an inner godly character should be a wife's primary focus.

Some wives, however, have gone overboard in the opposite direction, focusing all their attention on the inner person and none on the outer. There's nothing spiritual about looking like an unmade bed all day. A better balance—certainly one your husband will appreciate more—is to make your outward appearance a neat and attractive complement to your inner spirit.

The third brick for wives is called *attitude.*

> But let it be the hidden person of the heart, with
> the imperishable quality of a gentle and quiet spirit,
> which is precious in the sight of God. (v. 4)

The most attractive quality about a wife is not her outer beauty, but her inner attitude—which allows her spirit to manifest itself in two specific ways: gentleness and a quiet spirit.

Gentle carries the idea of genuine humility, and *quiet spirit* connotes tranquility. Peter is not saying that wives should be silent doormats. Rather, he's describing a woman of strong character and self-control. Someone who displays quiet elegance and dignity. Such beauty captures not only the hearts of men, but also the heart of God.

The fourth and final brick that Peter mentions is designated *attention*.

> For in this way in former times the holy women also, who hoped in God, used to adorn themselves, being submissive to their own husbands. Thus Sarah obeyed Abraham, calling him lord, and you have become her children if you do what is right without being frightened by any fear. (vv. 5–6)

The Greek verb for *obeyed* means "to listen or attend to another." It's the idea of paying close attention to someone. Sarah's response to Abraham was positive and helpful. She took the time to understand and be sensitive to his needs.

Wives, don't give away all your attention and energy to meeting needs outside the home. Start within the home, with your husband. Pay attention to him, take the time to listen and respond to his needs first.

Few things will deepen a relationship like this one brick. It will enable you not only to know your husband in an intimate way, but also to respond with wisdom and a great deal of understanding.

Now it's time for the husbands to step forward and receive the bricks Peter has for them. There are three, and they're all found in verse 7.

You Husbands . . .

> You husbands likewise, live with your wives in an understanding way, as with a weaker vessel, since she is a woman; and grant her honor as a fellow heir of the grace of life, so that your prayers may not be hindered. (v. 7)

The first brick seems to be a rather obvious one: *Live with your wife*. Staying in the same house, eating the same meals, and sharing the same bed, however, are not all that Peter has in mind here. The Greek term for *live* means "to dwell together," and it suggests being closely aligned or intimately familiar with one another. In addition, the preposition *with* reinforces the idea of togetherness and close companionship. Therefore, it is the husband's task to promote and maintain harmony and intimacy in the marriage relationship.

The second brick for husbands is *know your wife*. How? "In an understanding way." In Greek, that phrase reads, "dwell together according to knowledge." Husbands, listen to what she's saying. Be sensitive to her cares and concerns. Consider the pressures she lives under. Take the time and initiative to discover her fears, desires, plans, and feelings. That's the kind of openness and involvement that it takes to know your wife. And it is also one of the major ways husbands demonstrate their love to their wives.

The third and final brick Peter offers husbands is *honor your wife*. In Greek, the term for *grant* means "to assign." Husbands, you are assigned to nurture and uphold your wife's honor. And that includes far more than just treating her with the best of manners, although that is a good start.

For a clue as to how deeply we're to honor our wives, note that the same word for *honor* used here is translated "precious" when it describes the blood of Christ in 1 Peter 1:19. Both terms share the same Greek root. The idea is that a husband is to consider his wife a priceless gift, a precious treasure worthy of the highest esteem.

Husbands, have you assigned that kind of honor to your wives? Do they see it not only in your words, but in your actions? Does she sense that you treasure her? Or are you giving more affection and honor to a hobby, sport, or job?

Mixing the Mortar That Secures Each Brick

The bricks Peter has given us are essential for building strong, lasting, secure marriages. But one more thing is needed—mortar. Bricks alone cannot build a home. We need the godly traits Peter mentions in verses 8–9 to cement the bricks in place as we build.

> To sum up, let all be harmonious, sympathetic, brotherly, kindhearted, and humble in spirit; not returning evil for evil, or insult for insult, but giving a blessing instead; for you were called for the very purpose that you might inherit a blessing.

Take a brief look at the specific ingredients that cement the husband and wife together.

- Harmonious—"of one mind . . . in unity together."

- Sympathetic—"moved with concern for the other."

- Brotherly—"affectionate . . . warm and loving."

39

- Kindhearted—"compassionate."

- Humble in spirit—"humble-minded . . . unselfish."

- Not retaliatory or argumentative—"without a reactionary spirit."

When not properly mixed, mortar can easily crumble and fail to hold the bricks together. Are any of these ingredients lacking in the mortar that you're using to hold your marriage together?

Marriage may be difficult, and happy marriages may even be rare, but the fact is, they aren't impossible. God has laid the groundwork; He's drawn up the plans and even provided us with the necessary materials. Just how "happily ever after" our marriages become, though, depends on what we do with the plans and materials we've been given.

Everybody knows that Snow White and the Prince got married—and—lived happily ever after. What will be the rest of your story? They got married and . . .

 Living Insights

Building a marriage out the kind of bricks the apostle Peter talks about isn't easy. For most of us, all the training that we bring to the task comes from having watched our own parents build their marriage. It was there, growing up in the family, that we received our apprenticeship in bricklaying.

Wives, take some time to reflect on the role your mother filled when you were growing up. What "bricks" did she live out in the home? Use the following space to write your answers and expand on how her life left you prepared or unprepared to model the four bricks studied in our lesson.

_____

_____

_____

_____

_____

_____

So often we forget to think about the hard work that our parents put into their marriages. In looking back, was there a particular trait Peter mentioned that your mother exemplified? This week, would you offer her some thanks and appreciation for imparting that trait to you with her life?

Now, husbands, think back about your fathers. Did they fulfill the role of adoration? Of the three traits Peter talked about, which did they exhibit? How? In addition to answering these questions, give your overall opinion of how your father's life left you prepared or unprepared to build a strong marriage.

_____

_____

_____

_____

_____

_____

_____

The Scriptures teach, "The laborer is worthy of his wages" (1 Tim. 5:18b)—and certainly that would include fathers who labored hard and are worthy of receiving the heartfelt wage of gratitude from their sons.

Based on your reflections, choose at least one trait and call, write, or visit your father this week and thank him for the powerful legacy of that important trait. Let him know not only how it impacted your life, but also how it is making a positive impact in your marriage.

 Living Insights

To prepare for this next Living Insight, answer the questions listed under the appropriate section.

For Husbands Only

Of the four "bricks" that we studied for the wife, at which one does your wife excel? Give examples.

_____

_____

_____

Of the three traits listed for the husband, which do you feel is
your weakest? Why?

_____

_____

_____

For Wives Only

Of the three "bricks" Peter used to describe the husband, which
one does your husband do best? Can you think of some specific
examples?

_____

_____

_____

As you studied the four traits—actions, adornment, attitude,
and attention—which do you feel is your weakest area? Why?

_____

_____

_____

———————◆———————

Once the preceding questions have been answered, set aside
some time when the two of you can discuss them using this following
procedure: affirmation, admission, and alteration.

First, let the wife affirm the trait from 1 Peter 3:7 that she feels
her husband is strongest in. Following that, have the husband share
what he thinks is his weakest area and why. Then spend some time
brainstorming specific changes that could be made and write them
down.

_____

_____

_____

_____

_____

Next, reverse the pattern. Let the husband affirm a specific trait from 1 Peter 3:1–6 concerning his wife. Then have the wife share what she feels is her greatest weakness and why. Last, discuss some ways this area could be made stronger and write them down.

_____

_____

_____

_____

Chapter 6

WATCH OUT FOR CHEAP SUBSTITUTES!

1 Peter 3:1–9

It's a little thing. I probably shouldn't even mention it. But, well, does it ever bother you when you read a label that says, "Genuine Veneer"? Something about those two words just doesn't seem to go together. It's like saying, "Genuine Fake." Does that mean there are such things as "Fake Fakes" out there that we need to watch out for?

It's easy to be fooled about what's real and what's counterfeit these days. So much has been artificially simulated, imitated, and substituted, who can tell the difference?

Cheap substitutes abound not only in the products we buy, but also in the behaviors we adopt. Take the bricks we looked at in our last lesson. Those are the real things, the genuine articles when it comes to building healthy marriages. But, like everything else, there are cheap substitutes we can buy into instead . . . if all we want is a brick veneer.

What do you want? A copy? A substitute? A genuine fake marriage that looks fulfilling but underneath is really dead and disappointing? Of course not. But it can happen if you're not careful about your building materials.

Let's return to the apostle Peter's brickyard in 1 Peter 3, this time to learn about some of the cheap substitutes we should avoid using in our marriages.

Substitutes Commonly Used by Wives

Remember, wives, what Peter said about your actions?

> In the same way, you wives, be submissive to your own husbands so that even if any of them are disobedient to the word, they may be won without a word by the behavior of their wives, as they observe your chaste and respectful behavior. (vv. 1–2)

The witness of a godly woman's behavior is a beautiful thing to see. And it can also be convicting—powerfully so. Especially to a husband who's strayed from the Lord. Some wives, however, aren't content to let God convict their husbands just through their actions. So they rely on other means to get results.

Substituting Secret Manipulation for a Quiet Spirit

A favorite substitute of wives who refuse to let God deal with their wayward husbands is the manipulation technique. The rationale for using this approach goes something like this: "He'll never come around, so I'll have to step in and make sure he does." Believing that, the wife then devises all kinds of manipulative schemes—crying, lying, baiting—in hopes of ultimately getting her way.

A classic biblical example of manipulation is Rebekah. She was determined to have her younger son, Jacob, receive her husband's blessing instead of her firstborn, Esau. And with skillful deception, she got exactly what she wanted (Gen. 27). Chaste and respectful behavior? Hardly. Rebekah's manipulations showed an amazingly calloused contempt for Isaac.

The wife who would build her marriage according to God's design must put away her own designs. Manipulation only fosters suspicion and disunity, never genuine respect and trust.

Substituting External Appeal for Internal Beauty

Peter's next instruction to the wife touches on her adornment and attitude.

> And let not your adornment be merely external—braiding the hair, and wearing gold jewelry, or putting on dresses; but let it be the hidden person of the heart, with the imperishable quality of a gentle and quiet spirit, which is precious in the sight of God. (1 Pet. 3:3–4)

If you remember from our last lesson, Peter is not saying that external adornment is wrong. Rather, he's simply contrasting it with something that is more significant—internal beauty. Some wives, however, reverse the emphasis and create a cheap substitute.

These wives use their external attractiveness to get their way and maintain control. The seeds for this kind of behavior are often planted early in a young girl's life by parents who focus almost exclusively on outward appearance. The result of being praised and valued for their physical beauty is that many young girls become what Cecil Osborne describes as narcissistic women.

> A narcissistic person is . . . unduly preoccupied
> with her face, her body, and often with her own
> interests, which she perceives as an extension of
> herself. . . .
>
> A narcissistic woman constantly seeks to be the
> center of attention. She seeks flattery and is engaged
> in a constant battle for popularity. She's sometimes
> a psychic scalp collector, flirting with men in order
> to prove to herself that she has not lost her attrac-
> tiveness. She uses men, including her husband.[1]

Wives, is your color-coordinated appearance a thin veneer cov-
ering an immature character? God says to let your emphasis be on
the hidden person, to adorn yourselves with the precious qualities
of the heart that will never fade.

Substituting Learning What Is Right for Doing What Is Right

Peter concludes his teaching for wives with an example from
the Old Testament.

> For in this way in former times the holy women also,
> who hoped in God, used to adorn themselves, being
> submissive to their own husbands. Thus Sarah obeyed
> Abraham, calling him lord, and you have become
> her children if you do what is right without being
> frightened by any fear. (vv. 5–6)

Look carefully at verse 6 where it says, "you have become her
children if you *do* what is right" (emphasis added). Sarah acted on
what she knew was right. However, for many wives today a substitute has crept in that replaces doing with learning.

This is perhaps the most subtle and common substitute in con-
temporary marriages. To be frank, wives, many of you don't need
to *learn* more biblical truth nearly as much as you need to *do* more.
You don't need another seminar, study group, or book to read.
Enough time and money has been invested in those things already.
What's needed now is simply applying what you've already learned.

Has this subtle substitute of learning more and more crept into
your life? Is your Christianity conveyed more by what you know
than by how you live? If so, follow Sarah's example and become a

---

1. Cecil G. Osborne, *The Art of Understanding Your Mate* (Grand Rapids, Mich.: Zondervan
Publishing House, 1970), pp. 150, 151.

doer of the Word and not merely a hearer who deludes herself (see James 1:22).

Now let's shift our attention to the men and look at the substitutes they're prone to use in marriage.

Substitutes Commonly Used by Husbands

The first cheap substitute husbands need to watch out for falls in the area of perspective.

Substituting Providing a Living for Sharing a Life

Peter begins his counsel to men with these words: "You husbands likewise, live with your wives" (1 Pet. 3:7a).

As we noted in the last lesson, "live with your wives" means more than just sharing the same roof. It suggests togetherness, intimacy, really knowing your wife. Many husbands, however, have married themselves to their jobs instead. They have substituted making a living for the making of a marriage.

Providing a living is not all there is to being a husband; that's just part of the basic responsibility. Remember, your wives didn't marry your paycheck—they married you. And they long to know the real you, to have you open up and share what you're thinking and feeling. Openness, honesty, vulnerability—that's what it takes to truly live with your wives. Which are you sharing: your life or your paycheck?

Substituting Demanding for Managing

Peter also exhorts the husbands to live with their wives "in an understanding way, as with a weaker vessel" (v. 7b).

Such living calls for wisdom and wise management. Unfortunately, many men, out of either insecurity or ignorance, replace managing with demanding.

To avoid that kind of cheap substitute with their wives, husbands must invest time in knowing their mates. They must learn how to manage the home so that the wife's security is nurtured, her respect built up, and her potential encouraged.

In his book *Christian Living in the Home*, Jay Adams provides a helpful, detailed description of the husband who manages instead of demands.

> Headship does not mean crushing a wife's talents and
> gifts. It does not mean making all of the decisions

47

without reference to her or the children, or giving to her no power to make decisions or to do anything on her own. Precisely the opposite is true of the Biblical picture. . . . The good manager will recognize that God has provided his wife as a helper for him. . . . He thinks of her as a useful, helpful, and wonderful blessing from God. She is a helper, and as a helper he will *let* her help. He will encourage her to help.[2]

Managing in this way involves attentive listening, sensitivity, compassion, and insight—none of which you'll find in the demanding husband's home. Guard against this substitute, men. It's abusive and will only build walls between you and your wives.

Substituting Smothering for Honoring

The final substitute for the husband to watch out for has to do with Peter's instruction to grant the wife "honor as a fellow heir of the grace of life" (v. 7c).

It's one thing to love and care for your wife; but it's something totally different to smother her with a possessiveness that's threatened by her desire to fulfill her potential. Jealous husbands suffocate their wives, treating them like prisoners under probation. Each evening the wife has to give an account of where she's been and with whom, what they talked about and for how long. Overprotective husbands, on the other hand, hover over their wives, never giving them the opportunity to voice their own thoughts and feelings.

True honoring is just the opposite. It involves showing your wives the respect and dignity they deserve by encouraging their personal growth and individuality. So, husbands, allow your wives the freedom to develop and minister in the unique ways God has designed for them.

How to Know if You Are Using Substitutes

To find out if cheap substitutes have crept into your marriage, evaluate the bricks of your relationship against the real things Peter lists in verses 8–9.

2. Jay E. Adams, *Christian Living in the Home* (Nutley, N.J.: Presbyterian and Reformed Publishing Co., 1972), p. 91.

> To sum up, let all be harmonious, sympathetic, brotherly, kindhearted, and humble in spirit; not returning evil for evil, or insult for insult, but giving a blessing instead; for you were called for the very purpose that you might inherit a blessing. (vv. 8–9)

Substitutes will have a very definite effect on these godly traits Peter has listed for us.

- Substitutes disrupt harmony, resulting in irritation.

- Substitutes stop the flow of sympathy, resulting in resentment.

- Substitutes hurt the free expression of affection, resulting in hatred and bitterness.

- Substitutes turn off kindness and humility, resulting in harshness and selfishness.

- Substitutes create the very things that Peter challenges us to put aside.

Today, far too many marriages could be described as having a "genuine veneer." Even marriages where the couple attends church regularly, leads Bible studies, smiles, and says, "Praise the Lord" a lot. They look solid, biblical, fulfilling; but underneath they're falling apart.

As you think about your own marriage, are there any cheap substitutes that need to be thrown out and replaced with the lasting materials the Lord supplies? If you want quality—something that will last and bring deep satisfaction—choose the right bricks!

 Living Insights   STUDY ONE

> The cruelty which is hardest to bear is often not deliberate but the product of sheer thoughtlessness.[3]

Sad to say, thoughtlessness is the cruelty that many husbands, myself included, are guilty of most. It's not that we cheat on our wives or beat them or deliberately shame them in public. Nothing of the sort. Instead, we just do nothing. That's our insidious offense, our sin against our wives. Sheer thoughtlessness.

3. William Barclay, *The Letters of James and Peter*, rev. ed., The Daily Study Bible Series (Philadelphia, Pa.: Westminster Press, 1976), p. 223.

We give at the office—our creative energy, our compliments, our courtesies—and then give nothing at home. We forget birthdays, do little or nothing on anniversaries, avoid entering into our wives' joys and pains, expect sensitivity but give little in return, rarely compliment, consistently show up late, and are only interested in our own dreams and goals.

What's really crazy is that we can do all those things and, simply because we don't cheat on our wives, still be thought of as good husbands!

A good husband according to God's standards, however, is one who grants his wife honor. He deliberately thinks about and plans ways of lifting her up, letting her know she's valued and respected.

Husbands, do you want to see your wife blossom and the love between you bloom? Grant her honor. Show her the kindness she deserves as a fellow heir.

In the space provided, brainstorm as many ideas as you can about honoring your wife. What would she appreciate? What communicates respect and worth to her? If you get stuck, ask your friends for ideas. If they don't know, have them do this Living Insight! And then keep asking others until you come up with at least fifteen specific ways of granting honor.

1. _____   9. _____

2. _____   10. _____

3. _____   11. _____

4. _____   12. _____

5. _____   13. _____

6. _____   14. _____

7. _____   15. _____

8. _____

Once you have your ideas, choose one that could be applied this week.

_____

Last, pray about this. Commit your plans to God, and ask that He use them to affirm your wife's honor.

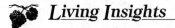

Wives, stop and think about the women you know who aren't Christians. By comparison, how would you say your knowledge of the wife's role in marriage stacks up against theirs?

Chances are that, unless you just became a Christian, your knowledge and understanding of the wife's role far exceeds your friends'. In fact, you're probably overloaded with biblical truths that you haven't even begun to process into practical living.

If you're not convinced, think about the last three marriage books that you read. What were they about? What specific truths did they present for you to apply? What have you applied?

_____

_____

_____

If you're like most, you've probably already forgotten a great deal about each of those books. Even though it may sound heretical, why not call a moratorium on buying any new books for awhile. Slow down on the number of Bible studies and marriage seminars you attend, and bring the focus in your life back to application. Give yourself more time to think through what you already know, to practice it so that your life changes, instead of just your knowledge.

What are some things you know you should be doing right now?

_____

_____

_____

Are you one of Sarah's children? This week, show this to your husband through your actions. Do what you know is right.

Chapter 7

WHO SAYS THE
HONEYMOON MUST END?

Genesis 2:25

When is the honeymoon over? The common cold is a good indicator. Art Sueltz humorously illustrates this by tracing the responses to a cold through the first seven years of a young couple's married life.

> The first year the husband says, "Sugar, I'm worried about my little baby girl. You've got a bad sniffle. I want to put you in the hospital for a complete check-up. I know the food is lousy, but I've arranged for your meals to be sent up from Rossini's. It's all arranged."
>
> The second year: "Listen, honey, I don't like the sound of that cough. I've called Dr. Miller and he's going to rush right over. Now will you go to bed like a good girl just for me, please?"
>
> Third year: "Maybe you'd better lie down, honey. Nothing like a little rest if you're feeling bad. I'll bring you something to eat. Have we got any soup in the house?"
>
> Fourth year: "Look, dear. Be sensible. After you've fed the kids and washed the dishes you'd better hit the sack."
>
> Fifth year: "Why don't you take a couple of aspirin?"
>
> Sixth year: "If you'd just gargle or something instead of sitting around barking like a seal."
>
> Seventh year: "For heaven's sake, stop sneezing. What are you trying to do, give me pneumonia?"[1]

We laugh not simply because it's funny, but because anyone who has been married for very long knows there's some real truth to that scenario. Unfortunately, what applies to colds also applies to the

---

1. As told by Bruce Larson in *The One and Only You* (Waco, Tex.: Word Books, Publisher, 1974), p. 20.

intimate physical affection couples share. In many marriages, the delight of sexual fulfillment erodes over the years until nothing of the exciting honeymoon passion is left. The physical pleasures that once fostered intimacy, joy, and love slowly disappear, leaving behind a businesslike nuptial arrangement from which neither partner receives much satisfaction.

Sound depressing? It is. But it doesn't have to be. Who says that the wonder of honeymoon oneness has to end? Certainly not the Lord. Not the Creator, who gave us our sexuality in the innocence of the Garden.

Review of Major Principles

When God presented Eve to Adam in Genesis 2, four foundational principles were established for loving, healthy marriages. We've already examined the first three principles—severance, permanence, and acceptance—in lesson 3. Remember that the husband and wife are to free themselves from parental control; they are to establish a permanent bond; and they are to nourish an accepting love that encourages a one-flesh experience of unity and personal growth.

Not only is each principle significant, but so is the order. Especially in light of the fourth and last principle: *intimacy*. For when the first three principles are present in a marriage, they establish a setting where intimacy—the kind described in Genesis 2:25—can flourish.

And the man and his wife were both naked and were not ashamed.

In Hebrew, the term *naked* means "to lay bare." It goes beyond describing physical nakedness to tell us that Adam and Eve were together in an open, unguarded, bare relationship. Their physical openness beautifully pictured the mental, emotional, and spiritual transparency they shared as well.

All of this, then—the principles, their order, Adam and Eve's unguarded relationship—made it possible for the intimate physical expression of their love to be enjoyed without any hindrances.

Biblical Facts about Marital Affection

To learn more about the sexual intimacy God intends to flourish in all marriages, let's look at five important facts.

1. *Intimacy in marriage was designed in innocence and was declared "very good."*

The first fact is found in Genesis 1.

> And God created man in His own image, in the image of God He created him; male and female He created them. And God blessed them; and God said to them, "Be fruitful and multiply." . . . And God saw all that He had made, and behold, it was very good. And there was evening and there was morning, the sixth day. (vv. 27–28a, 31)

From the very beginning, before sin ever corrupted this world, God established sexual intimacy in marriage (v. 28). The act of procreation and its enjoyment is by His design and He endorsed it as being "very good" (v. 31).

It is only after Adam and Eve sinned that God's design was exploited and perverted, resulting in shame and guilt. But we must remember, there's nothing wrong or depraved about sexual intimacy as God originally designed it for marriage. When enjoyed as He intended, it is still pure, right, clean, and good.[2]

2. *Intimacy in marriage was created not just for procreation but for personal pleasure.*

The second fact is based on Solomon's advice to his son in Proverbs 5.

> Let your fountain be blessed,
> And rejoice in the wife of your youth.
> As a loving hind and a graceful doe,
> Let her breasts satisfy you at all times;
> Be exhilarated always with her love.
> (vv. 18–19)

This is a beautiful expression of unrestrained sexual affection and enjoyment in marriage, a theme Solomon is even more eloquent and candid about in another of his books, the Song of Solomon. Listen as the wholesome ecstasy of marital love is unabashedly proclaimed in the wife's description of her husband, Solomon.

---

2. See also Hebrews 13:4, where we are admonished to protect the marriage bed—keeping it "very good" by preventing it from being defiled.

"Like an apple tree among the trees of the forest,
So is my beloved among the young men.
In his shade I took great delight and sat down,
And his fruit was sweet to my taste.
He has brought me to his banquet hall,
And his banner over me is love.
Sustain me with raisin cakes,
Refresh me with apples,
Because I am lovesick.
Let his left hand be under my head
And his right hand embrace me."
(2:3–6; see also 5:10–16)

Now listen as Solomon describes his wife.

"You have made my heart beat faster, my sister, my
bride;
You have made my heart beat faster with a single
glance of your eyes,
With a single strand of your necklace.
How beautiful is your love, my sister, my bride!
How much better is your love than wine,
And the fragrance of your oils
Than all kinds of spices!
Your lips, my bride, drip honey;
Honey and milk are under your tongue,
And the fragrance of your garments is like the fra-
grance of Lebanon."
(4:9–11; see also 7:1–9)

Both Solomon and his bride enjoyed one another—totally and completely. And God not only approved of it, He placed this passionate song of love and marriage in His Word so that others might learn from their example.

3. *Intimacy in marriage is planned for the husband and wife only.*

Crossing over into the New Testament, we'll find our third fact tucked away in the first two verses of 1 Corinthians 7.

Now concerning the things about which you wrote,
it is good for a man not to touch a woman. But because of immoralities, let each man have his own
wife, and let each woman have her own husband.

Having just read about the joys of sexual intimacy in Proverbs and the Song of Solomon, Paul, here, comes off sounding like a real killjoy. But he's not, really.

In studying the Scriptures, it's critical that we understand the context surrounding a passage. If we don't, it's easy to draw the wrong conclusions. Paul's point here is not to downgrade sexual intimacy in marriage. Rather, he's voicing his preference that men and women remain unmarried in order to dedicate their lives to the undistracted service of God (see vv. 32–35). For those men and women who don't have the gift of celibacy, however, Paul encourages them to find a mate—only one. The marriage ratio is one to one; one husband to one wife and vice versa.

4. *Intimacy in marriage is an expression of unselfish affection, not selfish desire.*

Continuing on in 1 Corinthians 7, Paul offers a perspective on sexual intimacy that may totally surprise some of you.

> Let the husband fulfill his duty to his wife, and likewise also the wife to her husband. The wife does not have authority over her own body, but the husband does; and likewise also the husband does not have authority over his own body, but the wife does. (vv. 3–4)

Husbands and wives, did you realize that physical intimacy in marriage was not meant primarily for your satisfaction, but for your mate's? Neither spouse is to selfishly withhold their body from the other. Instead, it is the duty of each to selflessly give of themselves so that both will experience joy and gratification. This incredible concept can, if you let it, revolutionize the sexual intimacy in your marriage.

5. *Intimacy in marriage is not to be interrupted except on very rare occasions.*

The fifth and final fact for us to examine is set forth in verse 5.

> Stop depriving one another, except by agreement for a time that you may devote yourselves to prayer, and come together again lest Satan tempt you because of your lack of self-control.

This tells you that sexual intimacy will be there in a healthy marriage whether it is in its first, tenth, or twentieth year, and it is not to be restrained except under certain conditions: *by mutual agreement* because of a serious situation that calls *for prayer*, and even then, *temporarily*. In other words, a break in the God-given flow of affection is to be the exception rather than the rule.

Some Reasons the "Honeymoon" Ends

If intimacy is such an important part of marriage, why, then, does the physical passion of the honeymoon slip away in so many cases? Let's briefly look at some of the causes and their cures.

One obvious cause would be physical illness or mental disorder. In either case, the help of a competent professional to work toward a cure is needed.

For some, the problem is simply ignorance—being uninformed about human sexuality. An easy way to overcome this is to pick up one of the many excellent books written by Christians which thoroughly discuss the topic.[3]

Still others struggle with marital intimacy because of tragic experiences in the past, such as rape or incest. In cases like these, it is often necessary to seek the assistance of a counselor who can help the injured spouse find healing.

However, a common cause of unfulfilled sexuality for a surprisingly large number of couples is simply boredom! Couples allow the expression of their physical relationship to become routine. Once in such a rut, the delight of marital love dies, which is why many husbands and wives are then easily tempted into extramarital affairs. What's needed is change, variety. Try a new technique, a new time, a new place. Why not take a weekend off, leave the children behind, and go on a "mini-moon" vacation?

In some marriages, the fire of sexual intimacy dies because certain habits develop that undermine the closeness of the relationship. Eventually, both the husband and wife become disinterested and retreat from one another physically. Something is wrong. The relationship isn't healthy. The need to find a solution must be faced squarely, and the necessary help sought.

One final cause found in many marriages is revenge. Spouses who have been hurt by their mates often withhold physical affection as a way of retaliation. Typically, all this does is cause the other

---

3. For help, read *Intended for Pleasure* by Ed Wheat, M.D., and Gaye Wheat (Old Tappan, N.J.: Fleming H. Revell Co., 1977), and *A Song for Lovers* by S. Craig Glickman (Downers Grove, Ill.: InterVarsity Press, 1976).

to feel hurt and pull away, which just results in the distance between the two growing wider and wider. In such cases, the cure needed to break this vicious cycle and restore intimacy is forgiveness. Reconciliation is essential to every marriage. Without it, the hurts and problems will continue to grow, causing the marital intimacy to quickly deteriorate.

Cliff Barrows once said that marriages are held together by twelve words: "I am wrong. I am sorry, please forgive me. I love you."[4] Simple words, but powerful. Powerful enough to keep your first love growing and to make your honeymoon last your whole life long!

 ## Living Insights

What is your goal in marriage? Are you committed to ministering to your partner? Do you love him or her with an accepting love that seeks that mate's best? Or is your goal really to manipulate your partner so that your needs, sexual and otherwise, are satisfied?

If our basic approach to our spouses is to take rather than give, we can expect to feel a lot of anxiety, resentment, or guilt. And, as Larry Crabb points out in his book *The Marriage Builder,* "these three troublesome emotions all tend to inhibit sexual arousal.

> It is difficult to feel angry with your spouse and sensual at the same time. If you are nervous around your partner, you will have trouble getting into the relaxed frame of mind vital to sexual interest. Similarly, a weight of guilt will block sexual excitement.
>
> It is fair to say that problems between partners that inhibit enjoyable sex can be traced to manipulative goals. . . .
>
> It obviously will do no good to instruct an angry husband, a worried wife, or a guilt-ridden partner to feel different. The remedy is to change goals. Shift from manipulating your spouse to meet your needs to ministering to your spouse's needs. When this shift takes place, these debilitating emotions slowly give way to compassion and warmth. Why?

4. Charles R. Swindoll, *Stike the Original Match* (Portland, Oreg.: Multnomah Press, 1980), p. 82.

1. The goal of ministering cannot be blocked by your spouse. There is therefore no trigger for *resentment* toward your partner;

2. Fulfilling the goal of ministry depends only on your willingness. The *anxiety* of wondering what your mate will do is eliminated.

3. The goal of representing the Lord to your spouse is reachable, at least as a basic direction. Although everyone occasionally fails, the resources of confession, forgiveness, repentance, and enabling are available to get back on the track and grow in consistency. There is no warrant for self-preoccupying *guilt.*

To remove problems to Body Oneness, people need to examine their moment-by-moment goals as they interact with their mates, confess wrong goals of manipulation, and set right goals of ministry.[5]

Let's do just that with regard to our goal of pursuing physical intimacy with our spouses. If anxiety, resentment, or guilt is present, could it be that your goal is to selfishly fulfill your own needs rather than to satisfy your mate's? After giving this some honest reflection, share with your spouse what you believe your basic goal has been—ministry or manipulation.

If the latter is the answer, take time for two things. First, confess that selfish attitude and ask for your spouse's forgiveness. Second, commit to a new goal of ministry. And to make this practical, talk through some specific ways you can approach and fulfill your spouse's needs for physical intimacy the way he or she would enjoy.

 Living Insights STUDY TWO

Oftentimes the joy of sexual intimacy in marriage ends not because there's manipulation, or conflict, or because the in-laws come to stay. Rather, it's simply because of carelessness, of neglect. Couples get caught up in busy schedules and inadvertently lose the time and energy it takes to cultivate the romantic physical intimacy they once enjoyed.

5. Larry Crabb, *The Marriage Builder* (Grand Rapids, Mich.: Zondervan Publishing House, 1982), pp. 96–97.

Has that happened to you? Are your days so full that your activities have distracted you from this one individual to whom you've committed yourself to love and cherish?

If so, use the following space to plan a time together for a "mini-moon" weekend or perhaps just an overnight getaway. Obviously, this would be just a beginning in reclaiming this aspect of your marriage. But perhaps during that time together, you could talk about how to make sure this tender part of your relationship gets the time and attention it needs to flourish.

Make plans now for the two of you to meet in a lovers' rendezvous!

Brainstorm Possibilities

Places and Times

_____

_____

_____

_____

_____

_____

_____

Make a Specific Plan

_____

_____

_____

_____

Chapter 8

TERMITES IN YOUR TROTH
Ephesians 5:13–21

Incredible as it may seem, the termite—a tiny, silent, unnoticed insect—causes more damage to buildings each year than fire. But which makes the evening news? The spectacular fires, not the insidious little insect.

This same thing is also true of marriages. Most homes aren't destroyed because of headline-type problems, but because of the quiet, inconspicuous irritations that eat away at a relationship year after year.

Speaking to his bride, Solomon cautioned against those pesky little aggravations by using a picturesque image familiar to his day.

> "Catch the foxes for us,
> The little foxes that are ruining the vineyards,
> While our vineyards are in blossom."
> (Song of Sol. 2:15)

The vineyard, representing the blossoming love between Solomon and his wife, must be protected against the small problems—the foxes—that could destroy their relationship if allowed to run free.

Foxes or termites, the analogy is the same: if not dealt with, seemingly harmless hurts and annoyances can eventually gnaw a relationship to pieces.

Exposition: Destructive Termites

For help in uncovering the termites in our troth,[1] let's turn to Ephesians 5, where the apostle Paul addresses a series of practical matters for Christians that easily relate to the husband-wife relationship. As we begin reading in verses 13–21, think in terms of marriage; and remember, it's the termites that we're looking for.

> But all things become visible when they are exposed
> by the light, for everything that becomes visible is
> light. For this reason it says,

---

1. *Troth* is an Old English word meaning "loyal or pledged faithfulness: fidelity." *Webster's Ninth New Collegiate Dictionary,* see "troth."

"Awake, sleeper,
And arise from the dead,
And Christ will shine on you."
(vv. 13–14)

Translating Paul's words into our analogy, imagine that he is telling us to inspect our marriages for termites, to expose to the light any destructive habits that may exist. He wants us to wake up to their insidious presence and listen to what the Lord says about getting rid of those pests! So in our time today, let's expose five of the more common species of marital termites that can weaken and ruin the relationship between a husband and a wife.

The "Confused" Termite

The first termite that bores its way into many marriages is found in verse 15.

> Therefore be careful how you walk, not as unwise men, but as wise.

To expose the termite of confusion, we must first dig a little deeper into the meaning behind three of the terms Paul uses. In Greek, the term for *be* means "to look." It carries the idea of discerning, observing, or taking heed. The following word, *careful,* means to do something with exacting or accurate requirements. The third term, *walk,* is used in the sense of conducting one's behavior. Paraphrased, all three communicate the thought, "Take heed, therefore, with great concern as to how accurately you are conducting your life."

Such a statement tells us that there is a standard by which we can accurately measure our walks. And that ruler is the Bible. Husbands and wives are to be exceedingly alert to how well their relationships square with God's Word. We're to be wise and walk according to the Scriptures, not unwise, stumbling around in confusion and ignorance.

Termites of confusion invade a marriage in three ways. First, they burrow their way in through intense propaganda against monogamous relationships. Marriage today is looked upon by many as being outdated and obsolete. God's design for the home has been largely discarded for makeshift philosophies that promise fulfillment and freedom but, in the end, engender nothing but hurt and disillusionment.

Another way this "confused" termite sinks its teeth into marriages is through the complexity of interpersonal relationships. For example, when a man and a woman are first married, they share a simple one-to-one relationship. Add one child, however, and the interpersonal relationships jump to three: husband to wife, mom to baby, dad to baby. Add another child and the relationships jump to six. Go to four and there are fifteen; five and you have twenty-one interpersonal relationships! In the midst of all these relationships is a wife and mother who often ends up wondering, "Who am I? A cook, a laundrywoman, a chauffeur, a plumber? Or a manager, financial planner, counselor, partner, or lover? Which one?" And similar confusion hits the father as well.

The third entrance for confusion is just plain immaturity. Many of us grew up *after* we were married. We weren't mature and our relationship wasn't mature when we jumped into one of life's biggest challenges. As a result, we've ended up stumbling over each other's feelings and causing each other pain in ways we don't even understand.

The "Busy" Termite

Did you know that, unlike other insects, termites never sleep? They just keep working, constantly tearing down—which describes our next marital pest, found in verse 16.

> [Make] the most of your time, because the days are evil.

Evil here means "being in active opposition to the good." That's how Paul characterizes the days in which we live. In light of that, his advice is that we make the most of our time.

The problem for many couples, however, is that they've fallen into the trap of becoming too busy. It's not that they're doing bad things, just too many things. The results are irritability, lack of communication, impatience, preoccupation, and feelings of distance. And that is an evil of its own kind. One that will undermine the intimacy and joy in any marriage.

What many of us need is to reestablish proper priorities. What we need is to manage our time better. What we need is to slow down.

> Slow me down, Lord.
> Ease the pounding of my heart by the quieting of my mind.
> Steady my hurried pace with a vision of the eternal reach of time.

Give me, amid the confusion of the day,
the calmness of the everlasting hills.
Break the tensions of my nerves and
muscles with the soothing music of the
singing streams that live in my memory.
Teach me the art of taking minute
vacations—of slowing down to look at a
flower, to chat with a friend, to pat a dog,
to smile at a child, to read a few lines
from a good book.
Slow me down, Lord, and inspire me to
send my roots deep into the soil of life's enduring
values, that I may grow toward my greater destiny.
Remind me each day that the race is not
always to the swift; that there is more to life
than increasing its speed.
Let me look upward to the towering oak
and know that it grew great and strong
because it grew slowly and well.[2]

Husbands, are you neurotically busy, always on the go, habitually tired, a workaholic? Wives, are you always hurried? Do you constantly run from one meeting to another? Are you nothing but a blur of activity day and night? That's not making the most of our time. That's being eaten alive by the termite of busyness.[3]

The "Dull" Termite

We can identify the third seemingly insignificant insect that gnaws away at our marriages by turning over the word *foolish* in verse 17 and looking at its meaning.

So then do not be foolish, but understand what the
will of the Lord is.

The original word for *foolish* in the Old Testament meant "dull, insensitive." It described something that was calloused and impervious to feeling. That same idea is being conveyed by Paul. Literally, he's telling us not to be thick, calloused, and therefore dull. Applying it to marriage, husbands and wives are to guard against becoming

---

2. Rev. Wilferd A. Peterson, as quoted by Tim Hansel in *When I Relax I Feel Guilty* (Elgin, Ill.: David C. Cook Publishing Co., 1979), p. 9.

3. If this describes you, read Tim Hansel's book *When I Relax I Feel Guilty*.

inconsiderate of one another. Don't let the "dull" termite tunnel in and cause you to adopt an insensitive, "I don't care" kind of attitude.

What can a couple do whose relationship is infested with "dull," indifferent termites? Paul gave us the answer in the second half of verse 17: "Understand what the will of the Lord is." In Greek, the word for *understand* means "to perceive, to be keenly aware and alert." It's the exact opposite of *foolish*. To rid ourselves of these termites, we must think keenly about our mates and our roles in marriage. We must become students not only of Scripture, but of one another.

The "Running" Termite

Still another species of marital termite is uncovered in verse 18.

> And do not get drunk with wine, for that is dissipa-
> tion, but be filled with the Spirit.

Extending Paul's meaning into our analogy, this represents the termite of running away, escapism.

Many escape the responsibility or pain they feel in marriage through alcohol. Others turn to food, drugs, work, social activities, hobbies . . . you name it. Just about anything can be used as a means of hiding or running from our spouses.

Paul warns that getting drunk—or any other excess, for that matter—will only lead to dissipation. The corollary for us is that every way out we try leads only to increased dissatisfaction. What we think are escape routes are really only dead ends. The way to deal with this termite isn't by running, it's by surrendering, by being filled with the Holy Spirit.

To avoid oversimplifying a difficult problem, let's make an important clarification. Paul is not saying, nor are we, that all a couple has to do is come to know Jesus and their marriage will be solid, immune to the kinds of termites we've described. Salvation doesn't come with any such guarantees. Instead, to guard against termites, a couple must be filled with the Spirit—meaning that they are under His direction, surrendered to His control. Instead of running to escape, the Spirit-filled husband or wife faces the problem by trusting in God's guidance and help.

The "Stubborn" Termite

The last termite we'll look at is the most subtle and common of them all. We'll find this destructive creature in verses 19–21.

Speaking to one another in psalms and hymns and spiritual songs, singing and making melody with your heart to the Lord; always giving thanks for all things in the name of our Lord Jesus Christ to God, even the Father; and be subject to one another in the fear of Christ.

To see the effect of the stubborn termite in marriage, think of the opposites of what Paul is saying here. Not melodic and harmonious (v. 19), but dissonant and disagreeable. Not grateful (v. 20), but resentful. Not humble (v. 21), but proud and selfish. These describe the stubborn mate who refuses to change or cooperate. "Wrong? Sure I'm wrong. But so is my mate! And if anybody is going to change, it'll be her, not me." Such a belligerent, bullheaded attitude turns holy wedlock into an unholy deadlock.

The stubborn termite feeds on self-centered pride, and there's plenty of that in all of us. So how can we conquer it? Through starving it by being subject to one another out of reverence for Christ. That's the secret.

Application: Pest Control

Even though we may never be able to completely exterminate the five termites we've identified in our lesson, we can control them by using the following three guidelines.

First, *admit their presence.* Honesty is the key. If marital termites exist in your home, confess them, bring them to the light. Exposure is the first step.

Second, *discuss all the possible ways to control them.* Whatever way you choose, it is going to involve sacrifice—because control costs. So when you make your plans, count the cost carefully. Make sure that both of you understand the plans and how they're to be carried out, lest you begin something that you are not able to finish.

Third, *start immediately—today!* The important ingredient here is discipline. Don't put off your plans until tomorrow or this weekend or next month. Start now by asking for the Lord's help in clearing these pests out of your marriage.

Because termites typically avoid sunlight, you rarely ever notice them until they've already caused extensive damage. Marital termites are like that too. By the time most couples become painfully aware of their presence, much has already been undermined in the relationship. So if we're serious about protecting our marriages against these pests, we can't afford to wait until they walk out and shake our hands. We've got to be on the alert so that we'll notice the very first signs of infestation.

To protect your marriage, take time now to conduct an on-site termite inspection by listing any signs you see of the pests studied in our lesson.

Termite Inspection	
The Termites	*Signs*
"Confused"	
"Busy"	
"Dull"	
"Running"	
"Stubborn"	

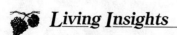

Of the five termites we exposed in our lesson, is there evidence of one in particular in your marriage?

_____

_____

Just as a way to bring this little, destructive critter out into the open better, is there another title you could give it that's more appropriate to your situation?

_____

_____

Spend some time with your spouse discussing and defining specific ways you can control this marital pest.

_____

_____

_____

_____

Finally, write down how and when you will implement these plans.

_____

_____

_____

_____

Chapter 9

HOW TO HAVE
A GOOD FIGHT

Ephesians 4:25–32

"The first nine years of our marriage were constant hand-to-hand combat," admitted one husband. If the truth were known, not some, but *most* marriages are marked by periodic skirmishes—and at times, all-out war! Some battles are night assaults. Others are surprise attacks. Still others are cold wars of stoic silence. Both sides may employ deadly tactics of public criticism, threats, intimidation, cutting sarcasm, or even physical abuse. Such maneuvers are common and *wrong*. Besides being unfair, they never lead to domestic peace, only to more pain and conflict.

In our lesson today, we want to make two general observations about marital strife and then examine seven rules that can turn an ugly fight into a wholesome, beneficial exchange that leads to peaceful resolution.

Round One: Basic Facts about Fights

Most couples don't really fight until after they marry, so they're inexperienced in dealing with strife. The reason for this is relatively simple. Everything before the wedding is voluntary. But after we say, "I do," everything is compulsory. Before marriage, we aren't obligated to deal with conflict. We can simply walk away. Afterward, however, honoring our commitment to one another involves staying and working through differences.

Compounding this problem is that instead of being open and real before marriage, many people play roles portraying only the things that will impress and attract others. Once married, however, the masks come off and for the first time real contact happens . . . and problems begin to surface.

Another fact about fights is that most aren't fair; therefore no one wins . . . both lose. In many marital conflicts, the only rule is that there are no rules. Both spouses feel free to use whatever strategy they choose. And, unfortunately, the choices are often unbiblical, dirty, and destructive.

Round Two: Rules to Fight By

All couples are going to have tiffs, spats, disagreements, fights, and a few hullabaloos in their time. It goes with the territory. But that doesn't necessarily mean that their marriages are unhealthy. Health isn't measured by the lack of problems, but more by the way we handle them. With that in mind, let's turn to Ephesians 4 and draw out seven rules that will help husbands and wives wage a clean, fair fight.

1. Be Committed to Honesty and Mutual Respect

> Therefore, laying aside falsehood, speak truth, each one of you, with his neighbor, for we are members of one another. (v. 25)

The verb *laying aside* is actually more properly rendered "having laid aside." It carries the idea of something already having been decided and done once and for all. So this first basic rule is a commitment, something already decided on in advance by both marriage partners.

Before the harmony in the relationship is broken by the next marital skirmish, the husband and wife should commit themselves to telling one another the truth. In light of our fair-fight context, it means saying, "Honey, no matter what, I want you to know that it is my deep desire to be honest with you and to respect you as a person."

The idea of respect comes from the last part of verse 25: "For we are members of one another." Christian couples are unique. Not only are they husband and wife, but they're also brother and sister—fellow heirs of eternal life. That adds another dimension to the marriage. Just as you hold fellow members of Christ's body in high regard, you should honor your marriage partner as well.

It is essential that you commit yourself to being honest in your marriage—ideally, before you begin your marriage—so that you don't fall into the trap of acting, of lying just to win your mate. A false life before each other breeds only lack of trust and disrespect.

2. Make Sure Your Weapons Aren't Deadly

> Be angry, and yet do not sin. (v. 26a)

Scholars commonly call this a permissive imperative. It means that instead of commanding us to blow our stacks, God permits us to be angry on certain occasions. With the same stroke of the pen, however, He warns us to not let that anger lead to sin.

When does anger become sin? Usually our consciences give us a clue: bursts of exasperated temper, for example. Anger that expresses itself in rage, lack of control, the desire to hurt another, or profanity. As Proverbs 18:14 reveals, this kind of fury is not only sinful, it is also deadly.

> The spirit of a man can endure his sickness,
> But a broken spirit who can bear?

When anger is out of control and abusive, it crushes the spirit. And that crushed spirit is not easily healed.

> A brother [or wife or husband] offended is harder to
>   be won than a strong city,
> And contentions are like the bars of a castle. (v. 19)

Now anger—when guided by reason, biblical principles, and a pure motive—*does* have a legitimate place in a relationship. What we're addressing here is the uncontrolled fit of temper or the bitter buildup to hatred whose deadly remarks wound, maim, and kill.

To be angry without sinning, we need to avoid three deadly tactics: (1) attacking the person instead of the problem, (2) rejecting instead of reproving, and (3) using gross exaggerations like "always" or "never." Each of these only intensifies the hurt, clouds the issue, and provokes the other's anger.

3. Agree Together That the Time Is Right

OK, so far a commitment of honesty and mutual respect has been established. Our weapons have been checked to make sure they're not deadly. Next, we *both* need to agree that the time is right to deal with the issue.

> Do not let the sun go down on your anger, and do
> not give the devil an opportunity. (Eph. 4:26b–27)

Paul is not only being specific about not letting anger build up day after day and night after night, he's urging us to use our time wisely. This would encompass an insightful sensitivity about timing, which highlights a most important word in our rule, *together.* Be sure both of you sense that it is the right time to talk. Don't jump into something the moment either of you drags home from work or when there's a stack of dishes and three children that need to be washed. Choose your timing carefully. Allow each other to say, "Honey, this isn't the best time," or, "This isn't the right place; let's deal with it a little later in a more appropriate setting." But when you say that, keep your appointment. Don't put it off. Don't let the day end with your anger unresolved.

4. Be Ready with a Positive Solution Soon after Taking a Swing

Although Paul deals specifically with the issue of stealing in this next verse, we can apply the broader principle to marriage. First, he confronts the issue: "Let him who steals steal no longer" (v. 28a). Paul leaves no doubt about where he stands—stealing is wrong before God. But notice that he comes right back with a positive solution.

> But rather let him labor, performing with his own hands what is good, in order that he may have something to share with him who has need. (v. 28b)

Condemnation without correction cripples the spirit. Instead of insensitively crushing people, Paul provides hope with a workable alternative. In the same way, as husbands and wives, do we simply crush with condemnation, or do we go on to offer positive solutions to problems?

5. Watch Your Words . . . Guard Your Tone

> Let no unwholesome word proceed from your mouth, but only such a word as is good for edification according to the need of the moment, that it may give grace to those who hear. And do not grieve the Holy Spirit of God, by whom you were sealed for the day of redemption. (vv. 29–30)

The term used for *unwholesome* means "rotten, worthless." It would include any kind of profane or bitter word. This will probably be the most difficult rule to implement because when we have a point to make that we feel strongly about, we tend to get louder. And the louder our tone, the uglier our words usually get, and the less our spouses can really listen. It's only when we speak softly, with respect, that we say more and are understood better.

A necessary ingredient for developing respectful and edifying communication in a marriage is tact. In his book *Family Communication*, author Sven Wahlroos offers this insightful definition.

> Tactfulness is an approach to another human being which involves being sincere and open in communication while at the same time showing respect for

the other person's feelings and taking care not to hurt him unnecessarily.[1]

Couples who lack this key ingredient in their marriage not only wound one another, but they also grieve the Holy Spirit (v. 30).

6. Don't Swing at Your Mate in Public

> Let all bitterness and wrath and anger and clamor and slander be put away from you, along with all malice. (v. 31)

Couples often take swings at each other in public, either with a bold uppercut of embarrassment or with below-the-belt jabs of sarcasm. Both punches hurt deeply because they humiliate, tearing the other's dignity to shreds.

So deal with your hurts in private, not public. If necessary, share them with a trusted counselor. But don't share them with the rest of the world just so you can win sympathy and support for your corner.

7. When It's Over, Help Clean Up the Mess

> And be kind to one another, tender-hearted, forgiving each other, just as God in Christ also has forgiven you. (v. 32)

This verse spells out three important bandages needed at the end of any fight. *Kindness:* at the heart of this word is grace. Be gracious enough to wipe this dispute off the mental slate. *Tenderness:* the root idea here is compassion. If your spouse is hurt from the fight, be compassionate enough to weep with him or her. *Forgiveness:* the word used for *forgiving* here conveys the idea of "doing a favor" for another. It's an exhibition of acceptance, the same kind of acceptance Jesus exhibited on Calvary. Freely give the forgiveness that Jesus has given you.

Round Three: How to Stop Most Fights

The way to stop most fights is actually very simple. When you are wrong, admit it. All it takes is three monosyllabic words, "I am wrong," or, "You are right." It's not complicated, but it isn't easy

---

1. Sven Wahlroos, *Family Communication* (New York, N.Y.: Macmillan Publishing Co., 1974), p. 159.

either. And we all know why—pride. It's remarkable what poor, stubborn, childish losers we can be because of our unwillingness to admit our mistakes. Yet when we do, when our spouse comes in all bent out of shape because of something we did and we say, "Honey, you're right, I shouldn't have done that," the fight is over before it ever began.

Issues will arise in all marriages, however, that may go several rounds before they can be resolved. When that happens, remember these rules and fight fair! Your marriage will be the winner if you do.

 Living Insights

When was the last time you fought, really fought, with your spouse? What was it about?

_____

_____

If you want to find out whether you fight fairly or not, go back over that recent conflict and measure it against the seven rules from our lesson. How did you deal with it? Were you honest? Under control? Did you offer a positive solution? To find out, rate yourself after each rule, with 1 being the lowest score you can give yourself.

- *Be committed to honesty and mutual respect.* How honest about your thoughts and feelings were you? Did you hold some back? Were you willing to admit when you were wrong? Was your response to your spouse respectful?

    1   2   3   4   5   6   7   8   9   10

- *Make sure your weapons are not deadly.* Did you attack the person instead of the problem? Were your words wounding, meant to harm? Did you resort to rejecting instead of reproving? Do you remember ever saying, "You *always* . . ." or, "You *never* . . ."?

    1   2   3   4   5   6   7   8   9   10

- *Agree together that the time is right.* Was your timing good? Were you sensitive to your spouse's needs in choosing a time?

    1   2   3   4   5   6   7   8   9   10

- *Be ready with a positive solution soon after a swing.* Did you condemn without offering any ideas for correction?

  1   2   3   4   5   6   7   8   9   10

- *Watch your words . . . guard your tone.* Were you tactful? Was your tone threatening or inviting? How constructive or destructive were your words?

  1   2   3   4   5   6   7   8   9   10

- *Don't swing at your mate in public.* Did you use embarrassment or sarcasm to belittle your spouse?

  1   2   3   4   5   6   7   8   9   10

- *When it's over, help clean up the mess.* How well did you apply the bandages of kindness, tenderness, and forgiveness?

  1   2   3   4   5   6   7   8   9   10

Living Insights   STUDY TWO

Now that you've seen some of your strengths and weaknesses in the way you handled a recent fight, look ahead to a future conflict that might be brewing now. Is there a particular issue that you need to discuss with your spouse?

_____

To prepare yourself to deal with this issue in a healthy way, go through each of the seven rules and write down what you need to do to obey each rule in approaching your spouse with this problem.

Be Committed to Honesty and Mutual Respect

_____

_____

_____

Make Sure Your Weapons Are Not Deadly

_____

Agree Together That the Time Is Right

Be Ready with a Positive Solution Soon after a Swing

Watch Your Words . . . Guard Your Tone

Don't Swing at Your Mate in Public

When It's Over, Help Clean Up the Mess

Chapter 10

'TIL DEBT DO US PART

Luke 19:11–26

Three phrases portray the financial portfolio of Mr. and Mrs. Average Couple: big bills—bank loans—and bad mistakes. Is it any surprise, then, that one expert wrote, "About nine out of every ten people with an income are financial failures"?[1] He doesn't mean they declare bankruptcy or have bad credit or don't make enough money. He's saying that they fail to manage their money wisely.

Ron Blue underscores this problem in his book *Master Your Money.*

> According to the Social Security Administration, only 2% of Americans reach age 65 financially independent; 30% are dependent on charity; 23% must continue to work; and 45% are dependent on relatives. Additionally, . . . 85 out of 100 Americans have less than $250, when they reach age 65. According to Devney's Economic Tables, fewer men are worth $100 at age 68 than they were at age 18—after 50 years of hard work. In other words, they have worked hard for 50 years and have not been able to save at least $2.00 each year. Why?[2]

Mismanagement. It puts not only our finances in the red but also our marriages. Couples with overdrawn bank accounts and bounced checks are rarely able to balance a home either. And eventually, their relationships become bankrupt and they dissolve their partnership through divorce.

There is a way to avoid losing everything we have invested in our marriages. God has given us ample principles in the Scriptures to guide us in the way we earn, spend, borrow, save, give, and invest money. Let's turn to Luke 19 and discover some of these biblical guidelines that can help us become wise managers.

---

1. George M. Bowman, *Here's How to Succeed with Your Money* (Chicago, Ill.: Moody Press, 1960), p. 86.

2. Ron Blue, *Master Your Money* (Nashville, Tenn.: Thomas Nelson Publishers, 1986), p. 13.

Biblical Facts That Correct Wrong Attitudes

Instead of getting into the prophetic significance of Jesus' parable in verses 11–26, we'll be focusing on the practical financial insights that it has to offer. In particular, there are seven biblical facts that correct seven wrong attitudes commonly held by married couples who are negligent in money management.

Fact 1: Everything We Have Comes from God

> And while they were listening to these things, [Jesus] went on to tell a parable. . . . "A certain nobleman went to a distant country to receive a kingdom for himself, and then return. And he called ten of his slaves, and gave them ten minas." (vv. 11–13a)

A mina was about three month's wages. It was an enormous amount of money, especially to slaves who never owned anything—not even the clothes on their backs. They were totally dependent upon their masters for all their provisions.

Like those slaves, we, too, are dependent upon our Master for everything we have, including our money. Many people, however, have the notion that only their tithe belongs to the Lord and the rest is theirs to do with as they like. Theirs is a "that part is God's . . . what's left is mine" kind of approach to finances. But that attitude is contrary to the biblical truth pictured in the parable. We are only stewards of what God entrusts to us, not owners (see also Deut. 8:11–18). And like the nobleman, the Lord expects us to invest His minas wisely, which leads us to our second fact.

Fact 2: Our Business Life Is Important to God

> "And [the nobleman] said to [his slaves], 'Do business with this until I come back.'" (Luke 19:13b)

The Greek word for *business* here is *pragmateuomai*, from which we get the word *pragmatic*. The master was extremely interested in what became of his money, enough so that he commanded his slaves to put his money to practical use.

Many Christians today believe that God isn't interested in "secular" things like business, only "spiritual" matters such as prayer, evangelism, and Bible study. Wrong! *All* of our life is important to God; there is no secular/spiritual distinction in Scripture. Everything is sacred!

Remember what Paul wrote? "Whatever you do, do your work heartily, as for the Lord rather than for men" (Col. 3:23). If you're a teacher, consider yourself a "teacher ordained of God." If you're a homemaker, you're an ordained homemaker. If you're an investment banker, you're an ordained investment banker. Our Master is just as concerned about how we spend, borrow, and make money as He is in how often we pray or read the Scriptures. There is no distinction, no dividing line in life where who we are and how we act becomes less important to Him.

But the truth that God is interested in the way we do business doesn't set well with everyone. In fact, as we shall see in the next verse, there are many who would prefer that God not get involved at all.

Fact 3: Doing Business God's Way Is Contrary to Man's Nature

> "But his citizens hated him, and sent a delegation after him, saying, 'We do not want this man to reign over us.'" (Luke 19:14)

Notice that it wasn't the slaves who complained, but the citizens. Some of the nobleman's subjects didn't want his lordship. They wanted to be able to conduct their lives as they saw fit. "Our lives are our own business! We don't want to be accountable to him."

Today that same attitude is expressed by many who say, "Let's not get fanatical—leave God at church." Inside each of us is a selfish, rebellious nature that hates being accountable to God. Some of us will tolerate giving God a grudging hour or so on Sunday mornings, but the rest of life we claim as our own business to conduct as we see fit.

From our next fact, however, it's clear that God considers our business His business.

Fact 4: Wise Management of Money Pleases the Lord

> "And it came about that when he returned, after receiving the kingdom, he ordered that these slaves, to whom he had given the money, be called to him in order that he might know what business they had done. And the first appeared, saying, 'Master, your mina has made ten minas more.' And he said to him, 'Well done, good slave, because you have been faithful in a very little thing, be in authority over ten cities.' And the second came, saying, 'Your mina,

master, has made five minas.' And he said to him
also, 'And you are to be over five cities.'" (vv. 15–19)

Notice what was uppermost in the nobleman's mind when he returned—business! He wanted to know what his servants had done with his money. And notice, also, the response of the first slave. He said, "*Your* mina has made ten minas more" (v. 16, emphasis added). That servant had the right attitude. "Not my mina, lord, it's yours. With your financial provision I was able to earn this much."

Was the master angry that he had invested the money? Of course not. He was delighted and rewarded the slave generously. Unfortunately, there are many Christians today who are suspicious of success. But nowhere does the Bible condemn making money as being evil. Certainly, the "*love* of money is a root of all sorts of evil" (1 Tim. 6:10a, emphasis added), but not necessarily the making of it.

The first two slaves' handling of money was right, as evidenced by their words, their obedience, and their reward from the master. A reward he withheld from the one servant who failed to "do business" as he was instructed.

Fact 5: Poor Management Greatly Displeases Him

"And another came, saying, 'Master, behold your
mina, which I kept put away in a handkerchief; for
I was afraid of you, because you are an exacting man;
you take up what you did not lay down, and reap
what you did not sow.' [The master] said to him, 'By
your own words I will judge you, you worthless slave.'"
(Luke 19:20–22a)

Some of us might think, "Wait a minute, nobleman. At least he didn't lose your mina." But the nobleman wasn't pleased that he just sat on it. That's not being wise. The money was to be used to earn more money.

Strangely, many Christians prefer to sit on their money like that third servant because they feel that having little is more spiritual than having much. But the Lord loves the poor *in spirit* (Matt. 5:3), and that may be either a poor individual or a wealthy one. Money, or the lack of it, doesn't determine one's spirituality.

The slave thought he had an adequate excuse for not investing his mina, but the nobleman exposed the ridiculousness of his excuse with a simple financial plan.

Fact 6: Management and Disciplined Planning Go Hand in Hand

> " 'Why did you not put the money in the bank, and
> having come, I would have collected it with inter-
> est?' " (Luke 19: 23)

Good question. And you'll notice that the slave made no reply.
He couldn't; the nobleman was absolutely right. Had the servant
attempted even a minimal amount of management and disciplined
planning, his mina could have at least earned interest. But he
attempted neither—and neither do many of us. Instead, we just
sail along with an "ignorance is bliss" attitude, hoping that one day
our ship will come in and all our financial needs will be miraculously
met. The truth is, though, that management without a plan is
frustrating, and a plan without discipline is a dream.

Management and disciplined planning go together. Even so,
that is no guarantee of success. Everyone has ups and downs, gains
and losses. The only difference is that good stewards learn how to
avoid making the same mistakes over again because of our seventh
and final fact.

Fact 7: Financial Losses and Gains Provide Eternal Lessons

> "And [the nobleman] said to the bystanders, 'Take
> the mina away from him, and give it to the one who
> has the ten minas.' And they said to him, 'Master,
> he has ten minas already.' I tell you, that to everyone
> who has shall more be given, but from the one who
> does not have, even what he does have shall be
> taken away." (vv. 24–26)

Like the bystanders in this parable, many of us feel that God is
being unfair when we see someone who is already wealthy receive
even more. "Lord, why don't you give that money to someone poor
instead?" But God doesn't choose favorites to whom He'll give
money. Rather, He blesses wise management while poor management typically results in less and less. There are laws and principles
for living that include spending, buying, borrowing, and investing
which not even God Himself will break except in a few miraculous
cases. Our need is to learn from the losses and gains we experience
and continue to grow as wise stewards of His money.

That need becomes all the more clear as you realize how few the years are that you actually have to earn money.[3]

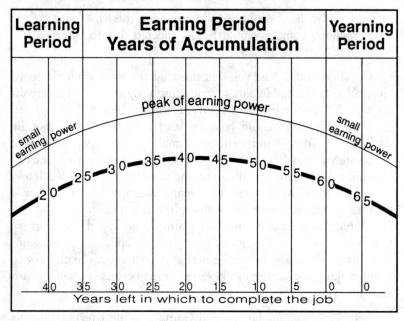

Learning Period	Earning Period Years of Accumulation	Yearning Period

peak of earning power

small earning power

20 25 30 35 40 45 50 55 60 65

small earning power

40 35 30 25 20 15 10 5 0 0

Years left in which to complete the job

In each person's lifetime there are three general financial stages. First, a learning period where we are hopefully trained by our parents about money management. Second, an earning period where we reach our peak earning capabilities. And third, a yearning period where we depend not so much on what we earn but on what we have saved.

How many years do you have left to plan wisely for yourself and your family? Look at it this way: When you're twenty, you have forty years left. When you're thirty, you have thirty years left. When you're forty, at the peak of your earning power, you have only twenty years left. By the time you reach fifty, you have approximately ten years left to plan your investments.

Negligence is a crime against one's own self and family (see 1 Tim. 5:8). The Bible offers us a wealth of sound, practical, dependable advice on money, which tells us that God is interested and that we need to be informed!

3. Chart adapted from Bowman, *Here's How to Succeed*, p. 86.

Scriptural Principles That Motivate Right Actions

For those of you who need help in becoming wise stewards with God's money, here are four sound principles you can take to the bank.

Christ and Caesar are essential . . . not optional. The first principle is found in Matthew 22, where the Pharisees asked Jesus if it was lawful to give a poll tax to Caesar or not. Jesus replied:

> "Show Me the coin used for the poll-tax." And they brought Him a denarius. And He said to them, "Whose likeness and inscription is this?" They said to Him, "Caesar's." Then He said to them, "Then render to Caesar the things that are Caesar's; and to God the things that are God's." (vv. 19–21)

It's interesting that this passage is frequently used to describe the biblical necessity of paying taxes, but seldom the importance of rendering to God the things that are His. And this slanted interpretation shows in the way many people give. A small part of their resources go to support God's church, and the rest is usually spent on building private little kingdoms here on earth.

As a married couple, have you thought through how you're going to give to the church just as carefully as you have planned to pay your taxes?

Buying and borrowing call for short accounts . . . not long. The second principle comes from Romans 13:8.

> Owe nothing to anyone except to love one another;
> for he who loves his neighbor has fulfilled the law.

What does that mean? Is it wrong to borrow, to take out a loan on a home or business? It would seem so, the way this verse has been translated into English. In Greek, however, Paul's command is actually given in the present tense: "don't keep owing." In other words, we're not to keep stacking up loans without ever paying them off. Debt must be paid as quickly as possible, not prolonged.

Savings and securities require planning . . . not hoping. If you're going to have a savings account to build up security for investment, you've got to do more than just dream—you need a plan. For those of you who aren't following any specific financial plans, here's a simple one to help get you started.[4]

---

4. Chart adapted from Bowman, *Here's How to Succeed*, p. 153.

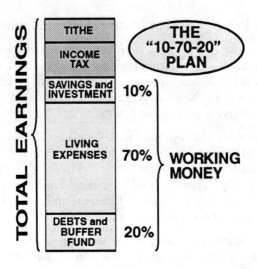

Out of your total earnings, the Lord comes first and then taxes to the government. The amount left falls under the category "Working Money." From that amount, allow 10 percent for savings and investments, 70 percent for living expenses, and 20 percent for debts and a buffer fund to handle unexpected costs.

Also, seek out sound financial advice from someone you respect or from good books on this matter.[5]

Things and treasure are temporal . . . not eternal. The final principle, found in 1 Timothy 6, brings a needed warning to all of us.

> And if we have food and covering, with these we shall be content. But those who want to get rich fall into temptation and a snare and many foolish and harmful desires which plunge men into ruin and destruction. For the love of money is a root of all sorts of evil, and some by longing for it have wandered away from the faith, and pierced themselves with many a pang. (vv. 8–10)

It's easy to become so caught up in the making of money that it becomes our god. The result is that we bow the knee to profit and greed instead of to the Lord. Our hearts become obsessed with

5. For further study, read Ron Blue's *Master Your Money* and *The Debt Squeeze* (Pomona, Calif.: Focus on the Family Publishing, 1989).

hoarding and protecting our material possessions. As a safeguard against that kind of attitude, remember these wise words from the apostle Paul.

> Instruct those who are rich in this present world not to be conceited or to fix their hope on the uncertainty of riches, but on God, who richly supplies us with all things to enjoy. Instruct them to do good, to be rich in good works, to be generous and ready to share, storing up for themselves the treasure of a good foundation for the future, so that they may take hold of that which is life indeed. (vv. 17–19)

 Living Insights STUDY ONE

Remember what your father told you about borrowing things? "Take good care of whatever you borrow, return it promptly, and, most of all, always give back the item loaned in as good as shape or better than you received it."

Pretty good advice. It taught you to be responsible and to respect other people's property. To this day, you probably feel that added obligation of caring for something that doesn't belong to you.

But how about the money God has given you? Do you feel that same sense of responsible stewardship about your finances? Think about it. Mentally most of us agree that everything we have comes from God. But does the way we handle our money really reflect that truth? Carefully consider the following three implications about God owning everything, and you'll have your answer.

———————◆———————

> First of all, God has the right to whatever He wants whenever He wants it. It is all His, because an owner has *rights*, and I, as a steward, have only *responsibilities*. . . .
> . . . I literally possess much but own nothing.[6]

Compare Paul's attitude reflected in 2 Corinthians 6:10 with the rich young ruler's in Matthew 19:16–22. Then ask yourself, Which attitude mirrors my own?

6. Blue, *Master Your Money*, pp. 19–20.

---◆---

> The second implication of God's owning it all is
> that not only is my giving decision a spiritual deci-
> sion, but *every* spending decision is a spiritual deci-
> sion. There is nothing more spiritual about giving
> than buying a car, taking a vacation, buying food,
> paying off debt, paying taxes, and so on. These are
> all uses of His resources.[7]

Do you *spend* money with the same sense of responsibility toward
God that you have when you *give* money? Or does your sense of
stewardship extend only so far as tithing?

---◆---

> The third implication of the truth that God owns
> it all is that you can't fake stewardship. Your check-
> book reveals all that you really believe about stew-
> ardship. . . . It reflects your goals, priorities, con-
> victions, relationships, and even the use of your time.[8]

Take a look at your bank statement from last month. What does
it reveal about your attitude toward money? Does it reflect the
goals, priorities, and convictions of someone who's a steward? Or
an owner?

 ## *Living Insights*

For those of you who realize that you've been operating with
the attitude that only part of your money belongs to God and the
rest is yours, financial consultant Ron Blue offers this practical step
toward giving God full control.

> List anything that you now possess, about which
> until now you would have said, "This is mine." Then
> return the ownership of it to its rightful Owner by
> a simple prayer of commitment, sign the deed, and
> date it.[9]

---

7. Blue, *Master Your Money*, p. 20.

8. Blue, *Master Your Money*, p. 20.

9. Blue, *Master Your Money*, p. 23.

Deed[10]

On this date I/we acknowledge God's ownership and my/our stewardship responsibility of the following:

ITEM	AMOUNT
_____	_____
_____	_____
_____	_____
_____	_____
_____	_____
_____	_____
_____	_____
_____	_____

Date _____ Signature _____

Signature _____

"You now own nothing," Blue writes, "and are prepared to be a steward."[11]

10. Blue, *Master Your Money*, p. 24.
11. Blue, *Master Your Money*, p. 23.

Chapter 11

COMMITMENT IS THE KEY
(PART ONE)
Selected Scripture

A merica—the land of plenty. A coast-to-coast cornucopia of abundance flowing with milk and honey. The Promised Land for the tired, the poor, the "Huddled Masses Yearning to Breathe Free."[1]

Centuries ago, Canaan was just such a place to Israel's huddled masses who yearned to breathe free from their bondage in Egypt. They were the tired, the poor, the homeless, the tempest tossed. Egypt's refuse. But then God sent Moses. And through him, the Lord delivered His children to the Golden Door of Canaan—the Promised Land flowing with milk and honey.

Before they took possession of it, however, Moses issued this sobering admonition.

> "Then it shall come about when the Lord your God brings you into the land which He swore to your fathers, Abraham, Isaac and Jacob, to give you, great and splendid cities which you did not build, and houses full of all good things which you did not fill, and hewn cisterns which you did not dig, vineyards and olive trees which you did not plant, and you shall eat and be satisfied, then watch yourself, lest you forget the Lord who brought you from the land of Egypt, out of the house of slavery. You shall fear only the Lord your God; and you shall worship Him, and swear by His name. You shall not follow other gods, any of the gods of the peoples who surround you." (Deut. 6:10–14, see also vv. 17–18)

Resonating in Moses' words are three warnings: Don't lose your uniqueness. Guard against erosion. Maintain your distinctive walk. In a word, he was concerned about their *commitment*. The affluence

---

This message was not a part of the original series but is compatible with it.

1. Walter B. Knight, *Knight's Master Book of New Illustrations* (Grand Rapids, Mich.: Wm. B. Eerdmans Publishing Company, 1956), p. 463.

and influence of the pagan culture they were about to settle in could easily distract them from their devotion to the Lord.

Today, the same is true especially in affluent America, a land where such caustic attitudes as permissiveness, irresponsibility, and escapism flow along with the milk and honey and undermine the Christian's commitment not only to Christ, but to marriage as well.

Review: Characteristics of Our Day

For a closer look at why so many Christians adopt a casual attitude towards their marriage vows, let's examine four common characteristics that work against commitment.

Public Opinion

This first condition is that of public opinion—Israel's Achilles' heel. Over and over again it kept drawing them away from the Lord who brought them out of Egypt. And it is no less powerful an influence over many believers today.

Basically, we're talking about peer pressure. We live in a society where public opinion is queen. Never mind what the Lord says. If "everybody is doing it," then it must be right. Ours is a morality of the majority. Unfortunately, as one historian said, "It's doubtful that the majority has ever been right."

Nevertheless, peer pressure continues to thrive. Why? Because it plays on one of our deepest needs, the need to be accepted. Then, too, it has a very loud, persuasive, and pervasive voice—the media. Every day we hear public opinion's siren voice beckoning to us over the radio, on the television, in the movies, newspapers, and magazines. Its powerful urgings can easily pull the unsuspecting away from God's values and shipwreck their faith . . . and their marriages.

Without a commitment to the Lord to anchor our marriages, we'll drift into the prevailing latitudes of public opinion, where divorce is not only tolerated, but embraced.

Accommodating Theology

Another condition that weakens commitment is the tossed-salad approach to Christianity. Rather than obey all of God's Word, many churchgoers pick and choose the verses they find palatable and ignore the rest.

The prophet Ezekiel preached to people like this and the Lord warned him of their hypocritical ways.

"But as for you, [Ezekiel], your fellow citizens who talk about you by the walls and in the doorways of the houses, speak to one another, each to his brother, saying, 'Come now, and hear what the message is which comes forth from the Lord.' And they come to you as people come, and sit before you as My people, and hear your words, but they do not do them, for they do the lustful desires expressed by their mouth, and their heart goes after their gain. And behold, you are to them like a sensual song by one who has a beautiful voice and plays well on an instrument; for they hear your words, but they do not practice them." (Ezek. 33:30–32)

The crowds loved listening to Ezekiel. But they had no intention of applying anything he said to their lives. They were just there for the fun, the entertainment of it all. And that same thing still goes on today. People prefer listening to practicing. Why? Because application involves commitment. And it's much simpler to alter our theology than it is to change our lifestyle. All it takes is a little rationalization or finding someone who will reinterpret a passage for us to make it fit what we want it to say. And, of course, there's always grace. People who refuse to submit to the Lord love to excuse their disobedience by calling on His grace. But, as the apostle Paul said,

What shall we say then? Are we to continue in sin that grace might increase? May it never be! How shall we who died to sin still live in it? (Rom. 6:1–2)

When it comes to marriage, God gives us grace to help us stay committed, not to provide an out when we've walked away from our marriages with no biblical justification.

Delayed Consequences

A third principle that works against commitment is found in Ecclesiastes 8.

Because the sentence against an evil deed is not executed quickly, therefore the hearts of the sons of men among them are given fully to do evil. (v. 11)

The Living Bible translates it simply, "Because God does not punish sinners instantly, people feel it is safe to do wrong." Many marriage partners feel it is safe to divorce for this very reason.

Frankly, this characteristic of the Lord is difficult to understand. Why would a holy God delay judgment? Why is a sinning Christian allowed to abandon his or her mate with few or no immediate consequences?

The Scriptures don't say. They do say, however,

> Do not be deceived, God is not mocked; for whatever a man sows, this he will also reap. (Gal. 6:7)

One sixteenth-century saint wrote, "God does not pay at the end of every day. But at the end, He pays."[2] Consequences will come, but in His timing, not ours.

Christian Approval

The last place you would expect to find commitment undermined would be the church. But that is exactly where the apostle Paul found it. Listen as he deals with the Corinthian church's lax attitude towards a brother committing incest.

> It is actually reported that there is immorality among you, and immorality of such a kind as does not exist even among the Gentiles, that someone has his father's wife. And you have become arrogant, and have not mourned instead, in order that the one who had done this deed might be removed from your midst. For I, on my part, though absent in body but present in spirit, have already judged him who has so committed this, as though I were present. In the name of our Lord Jesus, when you are assembled, and I with you in spirit, with the power of our Lord Jesus, I have decided to deliver such a one to Satan for the destruction of his flesh, that his spirit may be saved in the day of the Lord Jesus. (1 Cor. 5:1–5, see also vv. 6–7)

Such discipline is virtually nonexistent in many churches today. And its absence gives tacit approval to those who, without any biblical grounds whatsoever, walk away from their marriages. That's what bothered Paul. He was grieved not only because of this man's

---

2. Ann of Austria, as quoted by Charles R. Swindoll, in *Strike the Original Match* (Portland, Oreg.: Multnomah Press, 1980), p. 157.

sin, but because of the Corinthians' complacent attitude which allowed, even encouraged, him to continue sinning.

How seldom do we hear of churches disciplining those who wrongly break their marital vows. And that tolerance has helped foster a shallow view of commitment in marriage.

Redo: Response to Our Day

When you think about all the forces that work against marriage today, it seems no small miracle that any of us stay committed. It's not easy. But the blessed news, remember, is that we can overcome the eroding influences because "greater is He who is in us than he who is in the world" (1 John 4:4).

Since we devoted this entire lesson to studying four conditions that weaken commitment, in our next lesson we'll focus on four principles that strengthen commitment. For now, however, let's close with two essential principles that reinforce permanence in marriage.

First, *unconditional love.* Does your love for your spouse teeter like a seesaw on the little word *if*? "Honey, I'll love you *if* you make me happy," or, "*if* you always do well financially," or, "*if* you give me what I want when I want it." That attitude is incredibly demanding and selfish and is nothing more than self-love seeking gratification. Unconditional love, on the other hand, seeks to give, not take. It places the other's interests before our own. How can selfish, sinful people learn to love like this? Through Jesus. He can empower us to love His way—unconditionally.

Second, *maintain unbroken vows.* When you vow to love someone till death do you part, keep your word! Never allow divorce to even be an option. Your commitment to the Lord and each other is all you've got to protect your marriage. Don't let public opinion or accomodating theology or delayed consequences or misguided Christian approval weaken and destroy it.

 ### Living Insights

How strong is your commitment to your marriage? Are any of the four conditions we studied in the lesson undermining your willingness to work through whatever difficulties you may experience?

Perhaps you've viewed Christian approval as a safety net. Certainly many of us have. When things get rough at home and the hurt goes deep, it's easy to start thinking, "The church wouldn't have a problem with it. They didn't before when Bill and Sue got divorced. What do I have to worry about?"

Or maybe it's public opinion that works on your commitment when there's trouble. "What's the big deal about divorce? Everybody's doing it. Besides, look at the way she's treated you. Nobody's going to blame you for leaving her."

Do you have an Achilles' heel in your commitment? Take a moment to think back over the last two or three difficult times in your marriage. Were you influenced by any of the four conditions from our lesson? In what way?

Public Opinion: _____

_____

Accommodating Theology: _____

_____

Delayed Consequences: _____

_____

Christian Approval: _____

_____

 Living Insights   STUDY TWO

At one time or another, most of us have been tempted to bail out of our marriages. So what keeps couples together, especially during the hard times? Our marriage licenses? Hardly.

It's our commitment. That's what binds us together for better or for worse, for richer, for poorer, in sickness and in health.

To reinforce the permanence of your marriage, why not put the two essential principles from our lesson—unconditional love and unbroken vows—in writing. Fill in the following marriage certificate of commitment using your own words.

Nᵒ 67685

CERTIFICATE OF COMMITMENT

To all who shall see these Presents: Greeting:
Know Ye, These two persons are legally authorized
to celebrate the

RITES OF MATRIMONY

Husband

I, _____, do solemnly commit to_____

_____

_____

_____

_____

Wife

I, _____, do solemnly commit to_____

_____

_____

_____

_____

INSIGHT · FOR LIVING ·

In Testimony Whereof, we hereunto pledge
ourselves to one another on this the
_____ day of _____ 19__.

94

Chapter 12

COMMITMENT IS THE KEY
(PART TWO)
Selected Scripture

During England's darkest hours in World War II, it was a pudgy, cigar-smoking bulldog of a man who held that country together. While others whimpered about surrendering, Sir Winston Churchill resolutely championed winning. Listen to what he said in his first speech as Prime Minister to the House of Commons:

> Victory at all costs, victory in spite of all terror,
> victory however long and hard the road may be; for
> without victory there is no survival.[1]

Month after month, the Nazi Luftwaffe bombers devastated Britain's city blocks and buildings, but the Prime Minister refused to budge. Never once did he consider capitulating. Instead he tenaciously held to a simple philosophy summed up in six words: "Wars are not won by evacuations!"

That same philosophy is desperately needed today to win another war—one that is devastating the homes and lives of millions. Lester Velie writes,

> [There is] a war against marriage and the family.
> It is a shouting war waged in the press, on TV, on
> the lecture platforms.[2]

As we saw in our last lesson, there are powerful forces at work to overthrow our commitment in marriage. Each day, the casualty list mounts as couples surrender their marriages to the Enemy with no biblical justification.

But our homes don't have to be on that list.

This message was not a part of the original series but is compatible with it.

1. Sir Winston Churchill, as quoted in *Bartlett's Familiar Quotations*, 5th ed., rev. and enl., ed. Emily Morrison Beck (Boston, Mass.: Little, Brown and Co., 1980), p. 744.

2. Lester Velie, "The War on the American Family," *The Reader's Digest*, January 1973, p. 107.

Renew: Principles for Our Day

For those of us on the home front for whom evacuation is not an option, here are four principles, reinforcements from 1 Corinthians, that will help strengthen our commitment to fulfill our vows.

Christian Marriages Have Conflicts, but They Are Not Beyond Solution

The first principle deals with battles that occur *inside* the home.

> But if you should marry, you have not sinned;
> and if a virgin should marry, she has not sinned. Yet
> such will have trouble in this life, and I am trying
> to spare you. (7:28)

With compassion, the apostle Paul attempts to "spare us" the conflicts that are certain to occur in every marriage by suggesting we remain single (vv. 7–8). Since it is God's will that most of us do marry, however, disagreements are bound to happen.

Even in the best of homes, tensions, disagreements, and irritations exist because we're sinfully flawed humans. But the presence of problems in our marriages doesn't necessarily mean that we have horrible relationships with our spouses. Rather, it's how we handle those conflicts that largely determines the health of our marriages.

Some marital struggles are deep, lengthy, terribly complicated situations that need wise counsel to be reconciled. Yet God is committed to every marriage, no matter how difficult the problems. The question is, are we? Are we willing to stay and face the painful issues that, when faced, bring maturity and intimacy with one another and the Lord? Or are we going to surrender and walk away?

If our goal in life is to avoid pain, our marriages won't last. But if we're committed to Christ, to do His will, the good news is that by His grace no conflict is beyond solution.

Now some couples might still think, "We're both committed Christians, so why should there be any conflicts in our marriage?" Paul explains why in verses 32–35.

> But I want you to be free from concern. One who
> is unmarried is concerned about the things of the
> Lord, how he may please the Lord; but one who is
> married is concerned about the things of the world,
> how he may please his wife, and his interests are
> divided. And the woman who is unmarried, and the

virgin, is concerned about the things of the Lord, that she may be holy both in body and spirit; but one who is married is concerned about the things of the world, how she may please her husband. And this I say for your own benefit; not to put a restraint upon you, but to promote what is seemly, and to secure undistracted devotion to the Lord.

It may surprise some to realize that when they married, they gave up the privilege of undistracted devotion to the Lord. Why? Because they married a "distraction." And regardless of how spiritually mature that spouse is, all marriage relationships experience problems and require a great deal of devotion that might otherwise have been dedicated wholly to the Lord.

Working Through Is Harder Than Walking Out . . . but It's God's Way

The second principle that encourages permanence in marriage can be gleaned from a sampling of verses taken from our same chapter in 1 Corinthians.

Are you bound to a wife? *Do not seek to be released.* (v. 27a, emphasis added)

But to the married I give instructions, not I, but the Lord, that *the wife should not leave her husband* (but if she does leave, let her remain unmarried, or else be reconciled to her husband), and that *the husband should not send his wife away.* But to the rest I say, not the Lord, that if any brother has a wife who is an unbeliever, and she consents to live with him, let him not send her away. And a woman who has an unbelieving husband, and he consents to live with her, let her not send her husband away. (vv. 10–13, emphasis added)

The underlying message about marriage in these verses is clear: "*Stay! Don't leave. This is for life.*" Couples who are experiencing problems, however, are often nagged by the question, "Why is it best to work through our differences instead of simply walking away? Surely walking away is better. It's quick, less painful, and so much easier." Or so it seems at the time. But the truth is, there is every reason for staying committed to our spouses. Here are just four.

- First, committing to work through problems is the continual counsel of Scripture.

- Second, working through problems strengthens us spiritually. Escaping doesn't.

- Third, resolving our differences and staying committed is a powerful testimony to the public. Especially to those who look up to us as models.

- And fourth, in most cases, the children are seriously affected if the marriage is broken.

We can have all these reasons down pat in our minds, but if we still secretly entertain the option of leaving, chances are we eventually will. At first, we may only pull back from our spouses mentally and emotionally. But that usually progresses, in the end, to the actual physical separation of divorce.

Only those who bulldoggedly remove desertion as an option possess the kind of commitment it takes to work through problems and make a marriage strong.

Being Committed Is Not Demanding My Rights . . . but Releasing My Rights

The third principle deals with the issue of the husband's and wife's rights discussed in verses 3–4.

> Let the husband fulfill his duty to his wife, and likewise also the wife to her husband. The wife does not have authority over her own body, but the husband does; and likewise also the husband does not have authority over his own body, but the wife does.

The selfish nature in each of us doesn't enjoy hearing such strong words as "duty" and "authority" when it comes to the subject of giving up our rights. "I've got my rights!" husbands and wives shout at one another, each wanting their needs met first. But Paul says that our focus should be on meeting our spouses' needs. And even though he's only dealing here with the physical side of marriage, his counsel applies to all other aspects as well.

One of the greatest breakthroughs in marriage comes when both spouses release their rights in favor of putting the needs of the other before their own.

The Christian's Ultimate Goal in Life Is Not to Be Happy . . . but to Glorify God

If it were possible to set in concrete one great, all-encompassing truth from both our lessons about commitment, it would be this final principle taken from the last two verses of 1 Corinthians 6.

> Or do you not know that your body is a temple of the Holy Spirit who is in you, whom you have from God, and that you are not your own? For you have been bought with a price: therefore glorify God in your body. (vv. 19–20)

The ultimate goal in life for the Christian is to glorify God—not to pursue happiness or find fulfillment or be loved and appreciated by others. Those things are important and have their place, but they're not to take precedence over pleasing Him in everything we do. And it certainly pleases and glorifies Him when we remain faithfully committed to our spouses.

 ___Living Insights___   STUDY ONE

The glory of God or our own happiness—which are we trying to achieve? Are they mutually exclusive? Have we confused the two? These are some of the questions and issues Dr. Larry Crabb touches on in the following excerpt from the introduction to his book *The Marriage Builder.*

> A . . . flaw in our views of Christian marriage (and the whole Christian life) is *the appealing emphasis on becoming happy and fulfilled.* . . .

> In some circles, people warmly speak of fulfillment in relationships to the point where adultery, divorce, and homosexuality are acceptable if they enhance one's own sense of meaning. "I must be happy, *I* must express who *I* am. Don't condemn me to a life of limited fulfillment. Don't box me in with your legalistic morality. Let me be Me." . . .

> Does fulfillment have a place in biblical thinking? Of course. Each of us feels a deep concern for our own well-being, and this is as it should be. . . .

The crucial issue is not whether we should be interested in our own welfare, but rather how we believe our welfare is best served. Pursuing whatever path brings the deepest immediate sense of internal well-being appears to be a rather sensible strategy for finding fulfillment. But the Bible teaches that there is a way which—although it *seems* right—in the end leads to death: the tragedy of personal emptiness and desolation. Scriptures about dying to self, finding one's life by losing it, being crucified with Christ, and living only for Christ make it clear that realizing true fulfillment depends not on preoccupation with fulfillment but on preoccupation with knowing God through absolute surrender.[3]

How do you believe your welfare will be best served? Through absolute surrender to God? Or is it possible you've switched allegiances to pursue fulfillment instead?

If your answer is "absolute surrender to God," prove it. Pretend you're on the witness stand and give as many specific examples as you can of how you're pursuing obedience to Christ in your marriage. You may find this to be an encouraging and affirming exercise— or you may find you need more evidence.

_____

_____

_____

_____

If you had to answer "fulfillment," what is it that is keeping you from surrendering to God in your marriage? Explore and list your fears and reservations as honestly as you know how. Then hold them up to the light of Scripture and to the character of God. Are they justifiable or realistic? Place each one before God today and ask His help in resolving them.

_____

_____

3. Larry Crabb, *The Marriage Builder* (Grand Rapids, Mich.: Zondervan Publishing House, 1982), pp. 10–11.

He said, "It's not going to hurt anybody. We'll just get a divorce and go our separate ways."

But it did hurt somebody. Lots of somebodies. Like that young couple whose marriage was floundering. What they needed was assurance that all marriages have conflict and that theirs was not beyond solution. What they got, instead, was a stumbling block. "If he can't make his marriage work, there's no hope for us. Why don't we just walk away?"

And there were others, like the people he had discipled. People with whom he had prayed and studied the Bible. Not hurt them? How blind and selfish could a person be? Of course it would hurt. Had he been lying the whole time he talked about loving and obeying God? Those people had trusted him, loved him, opened their lives to him. And now he's walking away, violating everything he had taught, and it's not going to hurt?

His wife hurt. So did the kids. And then there were the neighbors, the church, the community, and the ministries he was associated with. And, oh yes, the Holy Spirit—He was wounded too.

"But she can't make me happy," he said.

What would you say? Step into this true story and respond to his last statement. See if you can weave the truths we learned from our lesson into your answer in the space provided.

_____

_____

_____

_____

_____

_____

_____

_____

Chapter 13

DON'T JUST GET OLDER, GET BETTER!

Ecclesiastes 12:1–7; 11:1–8

Growing old and growing up—the two are not necessarily synonymous. They don't always stay in step with each other. Why? Because growing old is as simple as breathing. It requires nothing but the passage of time. Growing up, on the other hand, requires active attention, effort, and discipline.

This is as true for senior citizens as it is for teenagers. Age doesn't automatically confer maturity. Sixty-year-olds can sometimes act as immaturely as sixteen-year-olds. They, too, may occasionally need the reminder to stop being immature and act their age.

We need to work hard to grow up not only as individuals, but also as couples. The relationship between the husband and wife must pass through many stages to reach maturity. In his book *Homemade Happiness,* author Wayne Dehoney touches on a crucial stage for the older couple whose children have finally left the home.

> When two parents wave good-bye to their last child, they are entering one of their most critical periods of marital adjustment. Two roads are open to them. They may accept the situation as life's good gift to explore new heights of marital happiness . . . . Or they may travel a road in increasing loneliness, bitterness and neurotic behavior.[1]

Basically, Dehoney is saying couples can grow up together or they can simply grow older. Those are the two roads. The latter is littered with thousands of divorces each year.

In our lesson today, we want to sell some home insurance to those of you who are facing that crucial juncture Dehoney describes. The kind of insurance needed to protect your marriage from growing older but not better. It's yours for the price of growing up. Let's

---

1. Wayne Dehoney in *Homemade Happiness,* as quoted in *The Marriage Affair,* ed. J. Allan Petersen (Wheaton, Ill.: Tyndale House Publishers, 1971), p. 402.

turn to Ecclesiastes and examine the policy Solomon offers for a marriage that will pay rich dividends the more it matures.

Insuring Your Aging

To insure that our marriages will get better as they get older, there are five policy guidelines from Ecclesiastes 11 and 12 that we should follow. Rather than begin in chapter 11, however, we'll start with chapter 12, where Solomon clearly reminds us that we're getting older with several stark portraits of aging and death.

Growing Older

Remember also your Creator in the days of your youth, before the evil days come and the years draw near when you will say, "I have no delight in them." (Eccles. 12:1)

Few people are more bitter and lonely than those who reject the Lord and turn against life. To guard against that, Solomon issues a strong command for us to remember the Lord through our growing-up years before the kind of old age sets in that he describes in verses 2–7. Let's examine these verses one by one, looking past the word pictures to their meanings.

Verse 2 continues the thought started in verse 1: "before the sun, the light, the moon, and the stars are darkened, and clouds return after the rain." Commentator Donald R. Glenn writes,

As clouds often block out the light of the sun, the moon, and the stars, so old age is a period of diminishing joy (light) and increasing gloom (dark), heralding the approach of the long night of death.[2]

What a gloomy thought! Verse 3 doesn't get any cheerier:

In the day that the watchmen of the house tremble, and mighty men stoop, the grinding ones stand idle because they are few, and those who look through windows grow dim. (v. 3)

2. Donald R. Glenn, "Ecclesiastes," in *The Bible Knowledge Commentary: Old Testament*, ed. John F. Walvoord and Roy B. Zuck (Wheaton, Ill.: Victor Books, Scripture Press Publications, 1988), p. 1004.

This verse depicts the physical miseries of old age . . . trembling limbs, bent back, teeth so few that eating is useless, and failing eyesight. Verse 4 and 5 fill in more discouraging details.

> And the doors on the street are shut as the sound of the grinding mill is low, and one will arise at the sound of the bird, and all the daughters of song will sing softly. Furthermore, men are afraid of a high place and of terrors on the road; the almond tree blossoms, the grasshopper drags himself along, and the caperberry is ineffective. For man goes to his eternal home while mourners go about in the street. (vv. 4–5)

Here we see deafness setting in and the familiar sounds being silenced, as well as insomnia beginning and the frustration of becoming a light sleeper. Worse, Solomon tells us of the problem of phobias that often develop with age. We become afraid of high places, big crowds, or of venturing out. Our hair turns as white as an almond blossom, and we hobble along in the crippling grip of arthritis. But that's not all. Verses 6 and 7 take us beyond mere irritations to disease and, finally, death.

> Remember Him before the silver cord is broken and the golden bowl is crushed, the pitcher by the well is shattered and the wheel at the cistern is crushed; then the dust will return to the earth as it was, and the spirit will return to God who gave it. (vv. 6–7)

These images are a little more difficult to understand. The broken silver cord refers to a stroke, and the crushed golden bowl denotes the impairment of an older person's reason. The shattered pitcher represents heart failure, and the crushed wheel probably alludes to circulatory problems. But after all this, the aging process finally reaches its ultimate and inevitable end—death. That's reality. Nothing we do can change that.

What we can do, however, is learn how to get better as we grow older, in our marriages as well as in our years.

Growing Up

The sobering picture of aging in Ecclesiastes 12 introduces the first policy guideline that will help insure the future health of our marriages: *live realistically.*

The fear of getting older motivates all kinds of foolish and immature behavior in people. For example, some older men attempt to deny their age by divorcing their wives of forty years to run around with women young enough to be their granddaughters. And then there's the grandmother who tries to hang on to her youth by dressing in chic clothes styled for a younger body. Both behaviors are silly, and everybody who has seen either example knows it.

Frankly, there's something dignified and beautiful about old age until it tries to be a teenager. One woman confessed, "The happiest day in my life was when I stopped trying to look twenty years younger than I am and decided to be myself."[3] That's living realistically.

But there's more involved than just that. Living realistically also means being sensitive to losing touch with our spouses as we get older. Danger signals such as poor communication, loss of compatibility, and difficulty compromising must be recognized and dealt with, not avoided. Then, too, the husband or wife who lives with the fear of getting older and less attractive needs affirmation from the other mate. The need for tenderness and understanding is essential.

For the second guideline, we go back to Ecclesiastes 11, where we will find the remainder of our policy: *give generously.*

> Cast your bread on the surface of the waters, for you
> will find it after many days. Divide your portion to
> seven, or even to eight, for you do not know what
> misfortune may occur on the earth. (vv. 1–2)

What does Solomon mean? Listen to the way this passage is quoted in the Living Bible.

> Give generously, for your gifts will return to you
> later. Divide your gifts among many, for in the days
> ahead you yourself may need much help.

. Solomon is clearly telling us to share our worldly goods, not hoard them. The happiest older couples are those that give generously. And the meaning here isn't limited to just finances, either. One of the most common mistakes made by senior couples is the failure to see how valuable they are as people! Individually as well as together, they possess a rich storehouse of experience that could be helpfully given away. Insight, wisdom, time, and talent—all

---

3. *The Marriage Affair,* ed. J. Allan Petersen, p. 405.

these are valuable commodities that could be shared with others through volunteer work, church ministries, community work . . . the opportunities are endless.

In another of his books, Proverbs, Solomon also said, "He who waters will himself be watered" (11:25b), meaning that as we stay in the mainstream of life by giving ourselves away, we too will be nurtured. It's when we pull back, close our doors, and sit in selfish silence that we shrivel into the most miserable of people.

Before we read further into our policy, let's pause for four admonitions on giving. First, don't fear the risk involved in "casting your bread upon the water." It's true, giving is risky; especially when it is ourselves that we're giving away and not just our money. But it's worth it. The alternative is selfishness, and that leads only to a death-like existence.

Second, don't expect an immediate reward. Ecclesiastes 11:1 says, "you will find it after many days." How many times have people invested their lives in others but then never lived to see the results? How often does it take years before a mother sees the fruit of her long hours of sacrifice for her children? You may not find immediate results when you cast your bread upon the water, so don't strain your eyes looking for them. Let the Lord lead you to them after the number of days He has ordained.

Third, don't give in only one area. Verse 2 tells us to "divide our portion to seven or eight." In other words, give of yourself and your possessions in a variety of different ways.

Fourth, don't hesitate—things could get worse later! Solomon reminds us that we don't know what misfortunes may occur in the future (v. 2). So don't wait to give, thinking things will get better: "I'll give when I make more money . . . have more time . . . am feeling better." Give now. Don't hesitate and lose the opportunities that you have for ones that may never occur.

Moving on, our third guideline for getting better as we grow older is found in verses 3–4. It brings us back to that portrait of aging we saw in chapter 12: *adapt willingly.*

> If the clouds are full, they pour out rain upon the earth; and whether a tree falls toward the south or toward the north, wherever the tree falls, there it lies. He who watches the wind will not sow and he who looks at the clouds will not reap. (11:3–4)

Solomon starts out by showing us the inevitabilities in life. But then he gives a word of counsel: those who become preoccupied with these inevitabilities will become lazy and inactive.

The lesson here for older couples who want more out of life than just rocking chairs to sit in and the weather to talk about is that they must learn to adapt willingly. Instead of becoming set, stale, and inflexible, woeful about the mounting evidence of their aging, the husband and wife should actively pursue meaningful accomplishments.

Four major poets who lived to be over eighty did just that, and they accomplished more the last decade of their lives than they did between the ages of twenty and thirty. William Gladstone took up a new language when he was seventy. At eighty-three he became the Prime Minister of Great Britain for the fourth time. John Wesley was preaching daily with undiminished popularity and power when he was eighty-eight. And Michelangelo painted his world-famous *The Last Judgment* when he was sixty-six.[4]

How much poorer would this world be if these people had stopped adapting to life and spent their later years discussing creaking knees and graying hairs?

The fourth guideline takes us into the uncertain future with a comforting word of advice: *trust fearlessly.*

> Just as you do not know the path of the wind and how bones are formed in the womb of the pregnant woman, so you do not know the activity of God who makes all things. Sow your seed in the morning, and do not be idle in the evening, for you do not know whether morning or evening sowing will succeed, or whether both of them alike will be good. (vv. 5–6)

Three times Solomon uses the phrase "you do not know" to emphasize the uncertainty of the future. It's that uncertainty that often paralyzes people as they get older, making it impossible for them to step out in faith and trust in the Lord. It's difficult to keep active and keep contributing when our faculties are failing and our sense of self-worth is slipping. It's frightening to try new roles once parenting is finished and wage-earning is a thing of the past. But God says, "Keep moving! Trust Me! I'll help you through the adjustments."

---

4. Based on *The Marriage Affair*, ed. J. Allan Petersen, p. 406.

The final guideline comes from verses 7–8a: *rejoice daily.*

> The light is pleasant, and it is good for the eyes to
> see the sun. Indeed, if a man should live many years,
> let him rejoice in them all. (vv. 7–8a)

These two verses point out how good it is just to be alive, to "live deep and suck out all the marrow of life,"[5] as Thoreau said. Growing old may have its difficulties, but don't let it rob you of your joy. Stay positive, give thanks, cultivate a cheerful heart by focusing on all the things there are to rejoice about.

Perhaps this guideline, even our whole lesson, is best summed up by this anonymous prayer from someone who saw the possibilities associated with growing old and prayed instead to grow up!

> Lord, Thou knowest better than I know myself
> that I am growing older and will some day be old.
> Keep me from the fatal habit of thinking I must say
> something on every subject and on every occasion.
> Release me from craving to straighten out every-
> body's affairs. Make me thoughtful but not moody;
> make me helpful but not bossy. With my vast store
> of wisdom, it seems a pity not to use it at all, but
> Thou knowest, Lord, that I want a few friends at
> the end.
>
> Keep my mind free from the recital of endless
> details; give me wings to get to the point. Seal my
> lips on my aches and pains. . . . I dare not ask for
> grace enough to enjoy the tales of other's pains, but
> help me to endure them with patience.
>
> . . . Teach me the glorious lesson that occasion-
> ally I may be mistaken.
>
> Keep me reasonably sweet: I do not want to be
> a saint. A sour old person is one of the crowning
> works of the devil. Give me the ability to see good
> things in unexpected places and talents in unex-
> pected people. Give me the grace to tell them so.
> . . . Amen[6]

5. As quoted by Joseph Wood Krutch, *Thoreau: Walden and Other Writings* (New York, N.Y.: Bantam Books, 1962), p. 172.

6. Dale Evans Rogers, *Time Out, Ladies!* (Westwood, N.J.: Fleming H. Revell Company, 1966), pp. 76–77.

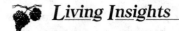

The first thing that all of us have to do when we take out an insurance policy is answer questions. Lots of them. For example:

Disorder of:			
1. a-☐ Eyes	b-☐ Ears	c-☐ Nose	
d-☐ Throat			e-☐ None of These
2. a-☐ Spine	b-☐ Back	c-☐ Muscles	
d-☐ Bones	e-☐ Neck	f-☐ Nerves (inc. Neuritis)	
g-☐ Joints			h-☐ None of These
3. a-☐ Fainting	b-☐ Convulsions	c-☐ Recurrent Headache	
d-☐ Dizziness	e-☐ Paralysis	f-☐ Stroke	
g-☐ Nervous Disorder	h-☐ Mental Disorder		i-☐ None of These
4. a-☐ Pneumonia	b-☐ Pleurisy	c-☐ Persist. Hoarseness	
d-☐ Emphysema	e-☐ Shortness of Breath	f-☐ Chronic Respiratory	
g-☐ Tuberculosis	h-☐ Persistent Cough	Disorder	i-☐ None of These
5. a-☐ High Blood Pressure	b-☐ Heart Murmur	c-☐ Heart Attack	
d-☐ Blood Vessel Disorder	e-☐ Rheumatic Fever	f-☐ Palpitation	
g-☐ Chest Pain	h-☐ Heart Disorder		i-☐ None of These
6. a-☐ Hemorrhoids	b-☐ Anorexia Nervosa	c-☐ Recurrent Indigestion	
d-☐ Intestinal Disorder	e-☐ Hepatitis	f-☐ Bulimia	
g-☐ Stomach Disorder	h-☐ Gallbladder Disorder	i-☐ Diverticulitis	
j-☐ Liver Disorder	k-☐ Recurrent Diarrhea		l-☐ None of These
7. a-☐ Kidney Stone	b-☐ Sugar in Urine	c-☐ Kidney Disorder	
d-☐ Pus in Urine	e-☐ Albumin in Urine	f-☐ Prostate Disorder	
g-☐ Blood in Urine	h-☐ Bladder Disorder		i-☐ None of These
8. a-☐ Diabetes	b-☐ Thyroid Disorder	c-☐ Endocrine Disorder	d-☐ None of These
9. a-☐ Allergies	b-☐ Leukemia	c-☐ Congenital Disorder	
d-☐ Anemia	e-☐ Blood Disorder	f-☐ Recurrent Infections	g-☐ None of These
10. a-☐ Sciatica	b-☐ Lameness	c-☐ Amputation	
d-☐ Gout	e-☐ Deformity	f-☐ Speech Defect	g-☐ None of These
11. a-☐ Skin Cancer	b-☐ Cancer	c-☐ Tumor	
d-☐ Fibroids	e-☐ Skin Disorder	f-☐ Lymph Gland Disorder	g-☐ None of These
Other Medical Information and Details			

And that's only one section of one page of one form! By the time you get through answering all the pages and pages of printed questions, and the fusillade of questions rattled off by an inspector over the phone, and a final burst of questions from a field representative that comes to your home to draw blood—then you're evaluated, thoroughly.

As important as it is for insurance companies to evaluate our physical health, it is also important that we carefully evaluate our marital health to insure that we're getting better as we grow older.

Set aside some time now to evaluate your marriage using the five (aren't you glad there are only five?) guidelines from our lesson. Have the husband pose the five guidelines to his wife as questions.

For example, "Do you feel that you give generously? In what specific ways?" And then reverse the roles and have the wife question the husband. Use your discussion as a brainstorming time, and make sure each spouse comes away with at least one action point to keep your marital insurance policy up to date.

 ## Living Insights

Is your marriage getting old and brittle? Has the freshness been replaced with staleness? The suppleness with stiffness? Vitality with boredom? Are you willing to adapt, to change, to try new things; have the same old routines become like sacred cows that you're unwilling to touch?

For many of us, it may be time for a sacred-cow roundup. We need to look at our marriages and see if we can identify those things that were once fun and exciting but have grown dull and routine. Do it now, and use the space provided to write down the "cows" you see.[7]

_____

_____

_____

_____

Now see if the two of you can come up with some new ideas to replace them. It doesn't have to be anything extravagant, perhaps even something as simple as taking a walk together. If you run low on ideas, ask some of your friends. There are plenty of creative, fun ideas for you to discover. As a start, you might consider putting that one-eyed cow called the television out to pasture for a while.

_____

_____

_____

_____

7. Charles R. Swindoll, _Living Above the Level of Mediocrity_ (Dallas, Tex.: Word Publishing, 1989), p. 293.

Chapter 14

WHAT TO DO WITH AN EMPTY NEST
Hebrews 5:7–6:1

All marriages go through seasons of change. "In the progress of a normal relationship," one author writes,

> a couple is continually encountering changing situations that demand a new orientation, a new pattern of reaction, a new way of facing life.
>
> Dr. Lofton Hudson has divided the progressive cycle of marriage into five stages: (1) family founding, from the wedding until the first child is born; (2) childbearing, from the birth of the first child until the first child enters school; (3) child rearing, when the first child enters school until the first child enters college or leaves home; (4) child launching, from the time the first child leaves until the last child leaves; (5) the empty nest, when the parents are alone until the death of one of the mates.[1]

In our lesson today we want to focus on that final stage—the empty nest. You would think that after working through the first four stages, most couples would readily welcome the last. But the truth is, many don't. Instead, feelings of dread and anxiety build as this final season of change approaches. For if the husband and wife have failed to nurture and protect their own relationship, the prospect of the children grown and gone can be a lonely one. Living in an empty nest with a stranger can be an empty feeling indeed.

Are there ways couples can adjust that will bring warmth and fullness of life into an empty nest? Yes, happily, there are. Hebrews 5, though not specifically about marriage, has practical dimensions that can be applied to couples whose children have finally left the nest.

---

1. Wayne Dehoney, "The Best Is Yet to Be" (Nashville, Tenn.: Broadman Press, 1963), in *The Marriage Affair*, ed. J. Allan Petersen (Wheaton, Ill.: Tyndale House Publishers, 1971), p. 401.

Exposition

The section of Hebrews we'll be studying can easily be divided into three parts:

(1) Christ during His earthly life (5:7–10)
(2) Christians (5:11–14)
(3) A command (6:1)

Let's carefully go over each of these passages, grounding ourselves in their meaning and their first-century context before applying them to the issue of the empty nest.

Christ

> In the days of His flesh, [Christ] offered up both prayers and supplications with loud crying and tears to the One able to save Him from death, and He was heard because of His piety. (5:7)

In just a few short words, we're given an anguished portrait of the Son of God who "in the days of His flesh," meaning His earthly life, sought the Father's strength. Doubtless, this must be a reference to Jesus' desperate agony in the Garden of Gethsemane. But if so, then it raises what appears to be a contradiction: why would Jesus pray to be saved from death if His purpose for coming in the first place was to die? Then, too, the verse says that Jesus' prayer was "heard," implying that it was answered; and yet we all know that Jesus died. Torturously so.

One very small Greek word, however, translated as *from*, untangles the thoughts for us. It literally means "from the midst of something." Jesus didn't pray to be delivered from death itself, but to come through it to the other side. He asked for the reality of the resurrection—to be brought back from the grave a conqueror over death and sin.

Continuing on, verse 8 immediately raises yet another issue that, on the surface, also seems contradictory.

> Although He was a Son, He learned obedience from the things which He suffered.

How is it that Jesus, who was God, ever needed to learn anything? Because even though He was in nature the very essence of God and therefore knew what obedience was, it wasn't until He became a man that learning obedience through suffering actually became a reality in His experience.

The last two verses in this section dealing with Christ's earthly life lift us from His anguish and suffering to His exaltation and promotion.

And having been made perfect, He became to all those who obey Him the source of eternal salvation, being designated by God as a high priest according to the order of Melchizedek. (vv. 9–10)

The key to understanding the author's meaning here lies in that first phrase, "and having been made perfect." It literally means "having been brought to completeness, brought to an end of that sacrificial experience." Once Jesus successfully completed His mission of salvation, He became the author and source of life to all those who believe in Him.

Verse 10 concludes with the Father "saluting" Jesus, another way of saying *designated,* by promoting Him to high priest.

Having painted this wonderful picture of Jesus' piety, obedience, and exaltation, the writer of Hebrews then turns his attention to the readers, who, in contrast to Christ, are disobedient and immature.

Christian

Concerning him we have much to say, and it is hard to explain, since you have become dull of hearing. (v. 11)

The "him" in this verse refers to Melchizedek in verse 9, who was a priest in the days of Abraham. The writer would like to go deeper and explain many significant truths about that individual and his order, but it would be useless, because the readers have become "dull of hearing." In Greek, that phrase means "sluggish and thick"; it's used to describe a limb of the body that has fallen asleep. The hearts and minds of the readers had become numb to learning. They weren't capable of responding to any new, profound truths.

For though by this time you ought to be teachers, you have need again for someone to teach you the elementary principles of the oracles of God, and you have come to need milk and not solid food. (v. 12)

Theirs was a problem of limited learning. They hadn't progressed beyond the "elementary principles," the ABCs of the faith. They should be taking in the mysterious depths of the Melchizedek priesthood, but instead, they needed to go back over the see-Spot-run basics.

Not only was their learning limited, but also their ministry. As long as they continued to need others to spoon-feed them, there was no way they could teach and encourage others who were new in the faith.

The third problem the author touches on concerning his readers is their limited discernment.

> For everyone who partakes only of milk is not accus-
> tomed to the word of righteousness, for he is a babe.
> But solid food is for the mature, who because of
> practice have their senses trained to discern good
> and evil. (vv. 13–14)

The readers lacked adult discernment because they did not practice the kindergarten-level truth they already knew.

Command

Even though in our Bibles there is a chapter break after that last verse, in the original letter no break exists. The writer immediately follows his painfully accurate description of his reader's limita-
tions with an exhortation to press on toward maturity—one which he applies equally to himself.

> Therefore leaving the elementary teaching about
> the Christ, let us press on to maturity, not laying
> again a foundation of repentance from dead works
> and of faith toward God. (6:1)

Be careful not to misinterpret this verse. The author isn't saying "Therefore, leaving Christ, let us press on." He says, "Let's leave the basics about Christ and get into deeper things." It's not deep when we leave Christ—it's heresy. But our knowledge about Him can and should go beyond just the details of the gospel. Just as the apostle Paul wrote to the Ephesians,

> So that Christ may dwell in your hearts through
> faith; and that you, being rooted and grounded in
> love, may be able to comprehend with all the saints
> what is the breadth and length and height and depth,
> and to know the love of Christ which surpasses
> knowledge, that you may be filled up to all the ful-
> ness of God. (3:17–19)

Application

Drawing from the truths highlighted in our passage from Hebrews, here are four helpful applications for those facing an empty nest either because the children have left or because a spouse has died or deserted.

1. *Renew your devotion to the Lord.* Even to the end of His life, Jesus renewed His devotion to the Father (Heb. 5:7). His agony in the Garden brought Him to the brink of death. Still, He refused to sit in silent misery. Three times He poured out His heart and reaffirmed His commitment in prayer (Matt. 26:39, 42, 44).

When you face that final, empty-nest stage, remember Christ's example. Renew your devotion to the Lord instead of sitting in self-pitying silence. Don't let any feelings of loneliness or abandonment deceive you into thinking God has abandoned you as well. He's there—always (Heb. 13:5). Jealously guard your times with Him during that difficult transition. Keep setting your mind on the things above (Col. 3:2). Jesus' prayers and weeping were heard because of His piety; let your reverence also be the megaphone through which God hears your supplications.

2. *Receive your situation in the Lord.* Jesus learned obedience from the things He suffered (Heb. 5:8). Many of us, however, never do. Why? Because we tend to fight the suffering that God allows in our lives. We refuse to accept and deal with difficulties. Our focus is on pleasing ourselves instead of obeying the Lord. And the life that focuses on itself becomes disobedient before long.

In contrast are those people who are beautifully obedient because their focus is on the Lord, suffering or no. As the empty-nest stage approaches, examine your focus. Is it on yourself or on the Lord? Have you accepted the situation God has for you? Are you willing to learn obedience, even if it means suffering?

3. *Realize your promotion from the Lord.* Once Jesus became the source of salvation through His death and resurrection, the Father promoted Him to high priest (vv. 9–10). We, too, when we cultivate a godly and obedient walk as Christ did, will find that the Lord will exalt us in ways that bring glory to Himself (1 Pet. 5:6). Ministry opportunities will open up that don't have to be manipulated or forced. Keep your eyes and heart open to discover the promotion God may be opening for you.

4. *Replace your limitations through the Lord.* Replace any limitations of learning, ministry, and discernment in your life by first confessing them. If need be, admit that you've been sluggish in your

thinking, or that you've been complacently satisfied with only the milk of the Word, or that you haven't been practicing your faith and lack discernment. Then ask God to strengthen you to "press on to maturity" in that particular area. And remember, the process of maturity is a marathon, not a dash. Limitations don't disappear overnight. It takes time for the fruits of the Spirit to ripen in each of us and fully replace the fruits of the flesh.

 ## Living Insights

How did your parents handle their empty nest? Ever thought about that? Their example could provide you with some important clues as to how prepared you may be to deal with this crucial stage in marriage. With your spouse, set aside some time to work through the following questions from the book *Passages of Marriage*.[2]

At what ages did you and your siblings leave home: Residentially (the day you moved out)?

_____

Financially (the day you no longer accepted loans from your parents, like down payments on a house)?

_____

List a couple of things your parents said as the first child left.
(*"Now that Bobbie's gone, we'll have peace again." "We're so proud of Bobbie; he's the first person in our family to go to college."*)

1. _____

2. _____

3. _____

What did your parents say when the last one left?
(*"I don't know what I'll do without Jane." "We're glad*

---

2. Frank Minirth et al., *Passages of Marriage* (Nashville, Tenn.: Thomas Nelson Publishers, A Janet Thoma Book, 1991), pp. 248–49.

Jane has found such a good job as a teacher and such a great apartment.")

_____

_____

Now think about what they did (their overt actions) when the first child left home. *(How many rooms formerly used by the children were converted to new uses and how many kept the same—"Still little Michael's room" when Michael left home five years ago?)*

_____

_____

When the last child left home. *(They converted your sister's room into a sewing room.)*

_____

_____

Now look for subsurface attitudes.

What indications, perhaps more felt than seen, tell you your parents made peace with their children's departure? *(They moved the dining room furniture around to better serve a close couple than to feed a mob.)*

_____

_____

Do any of these words or actions tell you that your parents never quite came to grips with their children's departure? *(Perhaps they left all your brother's sports posters up on his wall, or they refused to change anything in the house, just in case someone should come back home.)* ____ yes ____ no

The patterns your parents set will probably determine your own hidden agenda, the personal attitude your conscious mind doesn't even know about.

Assuming your children have not yet left home, what specific steps do you intend to take to avoid your parents' mistakes or rough spots?

_____

_____

What do you savor about the prospect of your children leaving home, whether it has occurred yet or not? (*I'll have more time to read or do some sewing.*)

_____

_____

And what do (did) you dread? (*[One woman] looked at her husband, sitting in the recliner and wondered what they had in common now that the kids were leaving.*)

_____

_____

 Living Insights _____ STUDY TWO

In another section of *Passages of Marriage* titled "The New Contract," the authors offer this creative idea which might be very helpful to couples needing to adjust and receive the situation of an empty nest.

Some of the old reasons to stay married have died, or, in the case of the children, moved out. As you forge a new contract, what are the new priorities and needs? . . .

Think about what would go into a renewal of your own contract at this stage of your marriage, whether you've actually reached this stage or not. . . . Go back through . . . your history together. Your particular situation is unique. What specific items might you write into a new contract to promote romance over the next years? What exactly can both of you do to avoid taking each other for granted?

118

Think about your history. What can you do to both deepen and transmit your family history and traditions? Write it all into the contract.[3]

Marriage Contract

_____

_____

_____

_____

_____

_____

_____

_____

_____

_____

🍇 *Living Insights*

We've come to the end of our study but not to the end of our work on our marriages. That work continues. But perhaps it's time for you to take a break and just look back at the good things that have been started or accomplished in your relationship. Perhaps you've opened up an area by knocking down a wall, or upgraded something, or added on a whole new dimension that you've never had before in your marriage.

Go back over the remodeling work done in the last fourteen chapters and write down at least three significant areas of improvement in your marriage. Then congratulate your co-worker and give him or her a hug! It might also be an appropriate time to thank the Master Architect for His guidance and strength in remodeling your marriage.

3. Minirth et al., *Passages of Marriage*, pp. 254–55.

Books for Probing Further

For further help in remodeling your marriage according to the Master Architect's plan, we recommend the following books.

Carter, Les. *Good 'n' Angry: How to Handle Your Anger Positively.* Grand Rapids, Mich.: Baker Book House, 1983.

Clark, Chap and Dee. *Let Me Ask You This: Conversations That Draw Couples Closer.* Colorado Springs, Colo.: NavPress, 1991.

Crabb, Larry. *The Marriage Builder: A Blueprint for Couples and Counselors.* Grand Rapids, Mich.: Zondervan Publishing House, 1982, 1992.

———. *Men and Women: Enjoying the Difference.* Grand Rapids, Mich.: Zondervan Publishing House, 1991.

Lewis, Robert, and William Hendricks. *Rocking the Roles: Building a Win-Win Marriage.* Colorado Springs, Colo.: NavPress, 1991.

Minirth, Frank and Mary Alice, Brian and Deborah Newman, Robert and Susan Hemfelt. *Passages of Marriage.* Nashville, Tenn.: Thomas Nelson Publishers, A Janet Thoma Book, 1991.

Wheat, Ed and Gaye. *Intended for Pleasure.* Old Tappan, N.J.: Fleming H. Revell Co., 1977.

Wright, H. Norman. *Holding on to Romance.* Originally published as *Romancing Your Marriage.* Ventura, Calif.: Regal Books, 1987. Reprint. Ventura, Calif.: Regal Books, A Division of Gospel Light, 1992.

We also recommend Family Life Conferences, sponsored by the Family Ministry of Campus Crusade for Christ, which are marriage enrichment and marriage preparation conferences where couples are equipped with proven solutions within a flexible framework that addresses the components of building a marriage. Topics include communication, conflict, leadership roles, sexuality, and intimacy. For more information, write Family Life Conferences, Post Office

Box 23840, Little Rock, Arkansas 72221-3840. Or please call 1-800-333-1433.

Some of the books listed here may be out of print and available only through a library. All of these works are recommended reading only. With the exception of books by Charles R. Swindoll, none of them are available through Insight for Living. If you wish to obtain some of these suggested readings, please contact your local Christian bookstore.

ORDERING INFORMATION

Cassette Tapes and Study Guide

This Bible study guide was designed to be used independently or in conjunction with the broadcast of Chuck Swindoll's taped messages on the topic listed below. If you would like to order cassette tapes or further copies of this study guide, please see the information given below and the Order Forms provided on the last page of this guide.

STRIKE THE ORIGINAL MATCH

As the newlywed years melt away in your marriage, is love's radiant glow growing stronger and more stable? Or is it dwindling to a dying flicker? Can you still feel the passionate flame that once blazed with hope and excitement?

Sadly, far too few of us can honestly answer yes. The warmth and intimacy we used to enjoy has been replaced by a cold distance. Why? Is it simply because we've fallen out of love? No. The real problem for many is that we have fallen away from the design for marriage God established with His first "match."

If this has happened to you, return with me to the guidelines of God's Word and rekindle your marriage. Let the Light of the world spark that trembling flame with His truth until it becomes a radiant blaze once again.

			Calif.*	U.S.	B.C.*	Canada*
SOM	CS	Cassette series, includes album cover	$42.36	$39.50	$60.31	$57.29
SOM	1–7	Individual cassettes, include messages A and B	5.36	5.00	7.61	7.23
SOM	SG	Study guide	5.31	4.95	6.37	6.37

*These prices already include the following charges: for delivery in **California,** applicable sales tax; **Canada,** 7% GST and 7% postage and handling (on tapes only); **British Columbia,** 7% GST, 6% British Columbia sales tax (on tapes only), and 7% postage and handling (on tapes only). **The prices are subject to change without notice.**

SOM 1-A: *Let's Consult the Architect*—Genesis 2:18–25;
Proverbs 24:3–4
B: *The Project: Let's Consider the Cost*—
Colossians 3:1–3, 5, 8–10
SOM 2-A: *Let's Repair the Foundation*—Genesis 2:18–25
B: *In Defense of Monogamy**—Selected Scripture
SOM 3-A: *Bricks That Build a Marriage*—1 Peter 3:1–9
B: *Watch Out for Cheap Substitutes!*—1 Peter 3:1–9
SOM 4-A: *Who Says the Honeymoon Must End?*—Genesis 2:25
B: *Termites in Your Troth*—Ephesians 5:13–21
SOM 5-A: *How to Have a Good Fight*—Ephesians 4:25–32
B: *'Til Debt Do Us Part*—Luke 19:11–26
SOM 6-A: *Commitment Is the Key (Part One)**—Selected Scripture
B: *Commitment Is the Key (Part Two)**—Selected Scripture
SOM 7-A: *Don't Just Get Older, Get Better!*—Ecclesiastes 12:1–7;
11:1–8
B: *What to Do with an Empty Nest*—Hebrews 5:7–6:1

*These messages were not a part of the original series but are compatible with it.

How to Order by Mail

Simply mark on the order form whether you want the series or individual tapes. Mail the form with your payment to the appropriate address listed below. We will process your order as promptly as we can.

United States: Mail your order to the Listener Services Department at Insight for Living, Post Office Box 69000, Anaheim, California 92817-0900. If you wish your order to be shipped first-class for faster delivery, add 10 percent of the total order amount. Otherwise, please allow four to six weeks for delivery by fourth-class mail. We accept personal checks, money orders, Visa, or MasterCard in payment for materials. Unfortunately, we are unable to offer invoicing or COD orders.

Canada: Mail your order to Insight for Living Ministries, Post Office Box 2510, Vancouver, British Columbia V6B 3W7. Allow approximately four weeks for delivery. We accept personal checks, money orders, Visa, or MasterCard in payment for materials. Unfortunately, we are unable to offer invoicing or COD orders.

Australia, New Zealand, or Papua New Guinea: Mail your order to Insight for Living, Inc., GPO Box 2823 EE, Melbourne, Victoria 3001, Australia. Please allow six to ten weeks for delivery by surface mail. If you would like your order sent airmail, the delivery time may be reduced. Using the United States price as a base, add postage costs—surface or airmail—to the amount of your order. Please use the chart that follows to determine correct postage. Due to fluctuating currency rates, we can accept only personal checks made payable in U.S. funds, international money orders, Visa, or MasterCard in payment for materials.

Overseas: Other overseas residents should mail their orders to our United States office. Please allow six to ten weeks for delivery by surface mail. If you would like your order sent airmail, the delivery time may be reduced. Using the United States price as a base, add postage costs— surface or airmail—to the amount of your order. Please use the chart that follows to determine correct postage. Due to fluctuating currency rates, we can accept only personal checks made payable in U.S. funds, international money orders, Visa, or MasterCard in payment for materials.

Type of Postage	Postage Cost
Surface	10% of total order
Airmail	25% of total order

For Faster Service, Order by Telephone or FAX

For Visa or MasterCard orders, you are welcome to use one of our toll-free numbers between the hours of 7:00 A.M. and 4:30 P.M., Pacific time, Monday through Friday, or our FAX numbers. The numbers to use from anywhere in the United States are **1-800-772-8888** or FAX (714) 575-5049. To order from Canada, call our Vancouver office using **1-800-663-7639** or FAX (604) 596-2975. Vancouver residents, call (604) 596-2910. Australian residents should phone (03) 872-4606. From other international locations, call our Listener Services Department at (714) 575-5000 in the United States.

Our Guarantee

Our cassettes are guaranteed for ninety days against faulty performance or breakage due to a defect in the tape. For best results, please be sure your tape recorder is in good operating condition and is cleaned regularly.

Note: To cover processing and handling, there is a $10 fee for *any* returned check.

Insight for Living Catalog

Request a free copy of the Insight for Living catalog of books, tapes, and study guides by calling **1-800-772-8888** in the United States or **1-800-663-7639** in Canada.

Order Form

SOM CS represents the entire *Strike the Original Match* series in a special album cover, while SOM 1–7 are the individual tapes included in the series. SOM SG represents this study guide, should you desire to order additional copies.

Item	Calif.*	Unit Price U.S.	B.C.*	Canada*	Quantity	Amount
SOM CS	$42.36	$39.50	$60.31	$57.29		$
SOM 1	5.36	5.00	7.61	7.23		
SOM 2	5.36	5.00	7.61	7.23		
SOM 3	5.36	5.00	7.61	7.23		
SOM 4	5.36	5.00	7.61	7.23		
SOM 5	5.36	5.00	7.61	7.23		
SOM 6	5.36	5.00	7.61	7.23		
SOM 7	5.36	5.00	7.61	7.23		
SOM SG	5.31	4.95	6.37	6.37		
					Subtotal	
			Overseas Residents *Pay U.S. price plus 10% surface postage or 25% airmail. Also, see "How to Order by Mail."*			
			U.S. First-Class Shipping *For faster delivery, add 10% for postage and handling.*			
			Gift to Insight for Living *Tax-deductible in the United States and Canada.*			
			Total Amount Due *Please do not send cash.*			$

If there is a balance: ☐ Apply it as a donation ☐ Please refund
*These prices already include applicable taxes and shipping costs.

Payment by: ☐ Check or money order made payable to Insight for Living or

☐ Credit card (circle one): Visa MasterCard Number _____

Expiration Date _____ Signature _____
We cannot process your credit card purchase without your signature.

Name _____

Address _____

City _____ State/Province _____

Zip/Postal Code _____ Country _____

Telephone ( ) _____ Radio Station ___ ___ ___ ___
If questions arise concerning your order, we may need to contact you.

Mail this order form to the Listener Services Department at one of these addresses:

Insight for Living, Post Office Box 69000, Anaheim, CA 92817-0900
Insight for Living Ministries, Post Office Box 2510, Vancouver, BC, Canada V6B 3W7
Insight for Living, Inc., GPO Box 2823 EE, Melbourne, VIC 3001, Australia